PENGUIN  CLA

SELECTED POEMS

PAUL LAURENCE DUNBAR (1872—1906) was born in Dayton, Ohio, to two former slaves from Kentucky. The family was poor and the father fled when Dunbar was two. Dunbar's mother, Matilda, supported her children by working as a washerwoman and by fostering in them a sense of the importance of education and a love of poetry. Dunbar began reciting and writing poetry in his childhood. The only black man in his class at Dayton Central High, he was a star pupil, editor of the school paper, and president of the school's literary society. While in school, he wrote for the *High School Times* and edited *The Dayton Tatler* along with his high school friends Orville and Wilbur Wright. When Dunbar graduated, he had difficulty finding a job appropriate to someone of his considerable education and worked as an elevator operator. Through mostly grassroots efforts and the help of friends, his reputation as a writer grew. His first collection, *Oak and Ivy*, was published in 1893, and that same year he was invited to recite at the Chicago World's Fair. There he met Frederick Douglass, who called him "the most promising young colored man in America." His second book, *Majors and Minors*, was published in 1895, and thrust him into the national spotlight when William Dean Howells praised it in *Harper's*. His first two books were republished professionally and he traveled to Engand to recite in 1897. He married Alice Ruth Moore, a young writer and teacher, who left him after a rocky relationship in 1902. Suffering from tuberculosis and depression, he died in 1906. He ultimately produced twelve books of poetry, four books of stories and plays, and four novels.

HERBERT WOODWARD MARTIN is professor emeritus and poet-in-residence at the University of Dayton. He received his M.Litt. from the Bread Loaf School of English at Middlebury College and his doctorate in creative writing from Carnegie Mellon University. The recipient of a Fulbright scholarship, he has published six collections of his own poetry and a collection of Dunbar's dramatic works. He performs Dunbar's poetry for audiences around the world and is the Paul Laurence Dunbar Poet Laureate for Dayton, Ohio.

PAUL LAURENCE DUNBAR

Selected Poems

Edited with an Introduction by

HERBERT WOODWARD MARTIN

PENGUIN BOOKS

14556484

PENGUIN BOOKS

Published by the Penguin Group

Penguin Group (USA) Inc., 375 Hudson Street, New York, New York 10014, U.S.A.

Penguin Books Ltd, 80 Strand, London WC2R 0RL, England

Penguin Books Australia Ltd, 250 Camberwell Road, Camberwell, Victoria 3124, Australia

Penguin Books Canada Ltd, 10 Alcorn Avenue, Toronto, Ontario, Canada M4V 3B2

Penguin Books India (P) Ltd, 11 Community Centre, Panchsheel Park, New Delhi–110 017, India

Penguin Books (N.Z.) Ltd, Cnr Rosedale and Airborne Roads, Albany, Auckland, New Zealand

Penguin Books (South Africa) (Pty) Ltd, 24 Sturdee Avenue, Rosebank, Johannesburg 2196, South Africa

Penguin Books Ltd, Registered Offices:
80 Strand, London WC2R 0RL, England

This edition first published in Penguin Books 2004

1   3   5   7   9   10   8   6   4   2

Introduction copyright © Herbert Woodward Martin, 2004
All rights reserved

LIBRARY OF CONGRESS CATALOGING IN PUBLICATION DATA
Dunbar, Paul Laurence, 1872–1906.
[Poems. Selections]
Selected poems / Paul Laurence Dunbar ; edited with
an introduction by Herbert Woodward Martin.
p.   cm.
Includes bibliographical references.
ISBN 0-14-243782-4
1. African Americans—Poetry.   I. Martin, Herbert Woodward.   II. Title.
PS1556.A4 2004
811'.4—dc22   2003061981

Printed in the United States of America
Set in Sabon

Contents

FROM LI'L' GAL (1904)

FROM LYRICS OF SUNSHINE
AND SHADOW (1905)

Introduction

Paul Laurence Dunbar had the paradoxical fortune to be born amid the influences of two movements that had enormous impact on what he wrote and how he wrote it: Romanticism, stemming from the European poetic tradition, and the rise of the minstrel, part of the American musical tradition.

The distinguished African American critic Charles T. Davis informs us in an essay entitled "Paul Laurence Dunbar" (in *Black Is the Color of the Cosmos: Essays on Afro-American Literature and Culture, 1942—1981*) that the Romantic tradition that held sway in the United States from 1870 to 1890 (121) is represented everywhere in Dunbar's work. Also of great influence is the minstrel tradition, which reached "its highest level in the decades between 1850 and 1870," according to Carl Wittke in his comprehensive study *Tambo and Bones: A History of the American Minstrel Stage* (64).

While the minstrel influences, found principally in Dunbar's dialect poems, may reflect a stereotypical view of blacks and slavery, his standard English poems depict a more Romantic view of the world. Reassessing those influences may shed refreshing light on why numerous critics felt it necessary to accuse Dunbar of being an accommodationist. The harsh reality that pervaded the end of the nineteenth century, with its attendant skepticism, may in some ways be attributed to the decline of the Romantic tradition. But more to the point, Dunbar seems to move back and forth between these two traditions while investing them with his own imagination and perception.

When William Dean Howells wrote his famous review of Dunbar's poetry in *Harper's* in 1895, he was for all intents and purposes introducing Dunbar to the American reading public.

Howells's statement contributed greatly to Dunbar's already growing reputation, and especially to the popularity of his dialect poems. Furthermore, he at once removed second-class citizenship from Dunbar and lifted the veil of obscurity that hung over African American talent. These are his words:

> . . . the contents of this book are wholly of his own choosing, and I do not know how much or little he may have preferred the poems in literary English. Some of these I thought very good, and even more than very good, but not distinctively his contribution to the body of American poetry. What I mean is that several people might have written them; but I do not know any one else at present who could quite have written the dialect pieces. These are divinations and reports of what passes in the hearts and minds of a lowly people whose poetry had hitherto been inarticulately expressed in music, but now finds, for the first time in our tongue, literary interpretation of a very artistic completeness.

Having calmed down from his newfound notoriety, Dunbar acknowledged Howells's generosity in a letter dated July 13, 1896:

> Now from the depths of my heart I want to thank you. You yourself do not know what you have done for me. I feel much as a poor, insignificant, helpless boy would feel to suddenly find himself knighted. I can tell you nothing about myself because there is nothing to tell. My whole life has been simple, obscure and uneventful. I have written my little pieces and sometimes recited them, but it seemed hardly by my volition. The kindly praise you have accorded me will be an incentive to more careful work. My greatest fear is that you may have been more kind to me than just.

However, while Howells's endorsement contributed greatly to Dunbar's fame and reputation, it also, inadvertently, created expectations about a stereotype of dialect. Often overlooked in Howells's praise is that he judged Dunbar's standard English poems "good and in some cases very very good."

Unfortunately, this endorsement went unnoticed by most of the editors who read the review. Instead they concentrated on Howells's assertion about the energy, power, and force in the tone and character of the dialect poems and generally ignored the high caliber of the standard English poems.

Concerning this question about dialect, Henry Louis Gates, Jr., has suggested in his book *The Signifying Monkey* that for

> . . . Dunbar to draw upon dialect as a medium through which to posit this mode of realism suggests both a certain boldness as well as a certain opportunism, two qualities that helped to inform Dunbar's mixed results, which we know so well, he lamented to his death.

Dunbar chose this avenue of "boldness" in order to gain, maintain, and secure his place in the American literary canon. There should be little doubt that Dunbar had an ear for perfect pitch. The rhythms and speech of his poems as well as the acquisition and approximation of that language testify to the "boldness" that he so readily took in hand and shaped into art.

For over one hundred years, readers have found an enormous amount of creativity invested in the dialect poems. There is truth in the critic's observation concerning the authenticity of voice in Dunbar's poems. A special humanity emanates from them, and when we admit this point, we must also admit that no one, including Dunbar, believed for an instant that African Americans were the perpetual happy dancers and singers of the stereotype while they suffered the yoke of slavery.

Howells, in his introduction to *Lyrics of Lowly Life*, observes:

> . . . Paul Dunbar was the only man of pure African blood and of American civilization to feel the negro life aesthetically and express it lyrically. . . . I thought his merits positive and not comparative; and I held that if his black poems had been written by a white man, I should not have found them less admirable. I accepted them as an evidence of the essential unity of the human race . . .

Howells is quick to take note of Dunbar's slave parentage. When it came to Pushkin, the Russians claimed it was his Russian genes that made him the great poet he became, and not his African ancestry; the same claim was advanced by the French when it came to Dumas. In the case of Dunbar, no such claim would be made. Dunbar had achieved for Africans and African Americans.

Because Dunbar longed for public attention for his work, the choice of entrance was clearly marked for him. The two doors read: Minstrel and Dialect. Dunbar gave in to the prevailing style and chose Dialect when it came to the poems and Minstrel when it came to the musicals and one-act plays. From another viewpoint it may be reasonable to understand why Dunbar and his future composer-collaborator Will Marion Cook arrived at the position they found themselves in if we consider a statement by Gary D. Engle in his book *This Grotesque Essence: Plays from the American Minstrel Stage* (xiii): "For better or worse, the characteristic art of a democracy is shaped by the will of the audience, not of the artist. Popularity becomes one measure of artistic value." Further, Engle sees the stereotypical, historical black as "that grotesque concoction of song, dance, wooly-wigged image of banjo-plunking, blackface minstrel clown" (xiv). In this regard Engle remarks that "The figure of the minstrel clown has been the most influential image of blacks in American history" (xiv). One might see, then, that this form and its use of dialect were inescapable.

Consider dialect as a tradition, and we have to entertain the four best practitioners of the art: Mark Twain in the South, James Whitcomb Riley and Paul Laurence Dunbar in the Midwest, and Bret Harte in the West. Perhaps most remembered and celebrated for southern white and black dialects, as well as standard English and "pretend" British English, are the Duke and King and other characters in *The Adventures of Huckleberry Finn*—often considered, ironically, the great American novel. No such honor is accorded Dunbar, but his use of dialect was not only on par with that of Twain but also equally memorable. Without his risk taking, American readers would miss the serious irony Dunbar employs in many of his dialect poems, and in many of his short lyrics as well. Whether or not we, in this century, endorse his choices, the irony remains that had he chosen differently, he would have had to struggle on in regional obscurity. His successes are due considerably to his willingness to make the "bold" choices and take the chances he did. Nevertheless, dialect proved to be the proverbial millstone around Dunbar's neck. It succeeded in trapping him in a genre that he slowly grew to hate. He says in a letter to Dr. J. N. Matthews: "*The Record* of Monday July 31st had a little poem of mine. They won't take anything but dialect so I have no market for anything else."

Ultimately Dunbar came to believe that Howells had done him irreparable harm in endorsing the dialect poems above those written in standard English. However, given the times in which Dunbar wrote, had Howells said nothing about his book, Dunbar might never have gained national attention. Howells gave Dunbar the recognition at the very time he needed it.

Nonetheless, dialect poetry was complicated by manifold issues, not only in terms of language, but also in terms of theme. The more sophisticated reader must have been stymied when he or she arrived at "Accountability," in which the narrator steals a chicken from the master's yard. The humor of his act is couched in predestination. He tells the reader that he is not responsible for his acts, and observes quite naturally that:

> . . . ef we'se bad we ain't to blame.
> Ef we'se good, we needn't show off, case you bet it ain't ouah doin' . . .

It is this characterization that landed Dunbar in trouble with the newly rising black middle class. They no doubt sought to prove themselves worthy of their new status by using what was considered proper English. Slaves, on the other hand, had acquired much of their English by ear. The laws of the times specifically forbade anyone to teach them how to read and write. How else was one to learn how to communicate, in this new foreign land, except by repeating the version of English

they heard from the people they were closest to? So dialect was
born. It is what contemporary society celebrates as vernacular.
What Dunbar was able to accomplish with dazzling singularity
was to hear the language as it was used and then approximate
that language and set it down in an artistic form. In the final
analysis, Howells was absolutely correct in his summation of
Dunbar's talent when he wrote: ". . . if he should do nothing
more than he has done, I should feel that he had made the
strongest claim for the negro in English literature that the negro
has yet made."

Furthermore, for all of the subjugation, ridicule, and mock-
ery that dialect suggests, there is in Dunbar a consistent ironic
tone even when the characters he presents seem to be mock-
ing themselves and playing the fool with the wink of an eye.
The rhythmic invention in "A Negro Love Song" anticipates
rap. Nothing is slight about the repetitive "Jump back, honey,
jump back." Rhythmically this line sounds like a Bach ground
for one of his inventions. The line also sustains the melodic
thought that runs throughout the poem:

> Seen my lady home las' night,
>   Jump back, honey, jump back.
> Hel' huh han' an' sque'z it tight,
>   Jump back, honey, jump back.

This is oral poetry at its lighthearted and humorous best. Its ef-
fectiveness lies in recitation. It must be read aloud. Indeed, the
persona in many of Dunbar's poems is asking to be freed from
the prison of the page. The poems are asking to be verbalized,
to take flight in the air. Dunbar seems to have been the best at
verbalizing the oral tradition in black American literature.

Nowhere is this oral tradition more apparent and effective
than in "An Ante-Bellum Sermon." The theme is freedom, but
it is couched in an analysis of the biblical relationship of the
Israelites and the Egyptians, and that is why the preacher says:

> . . . I'se a-judgin'
> Bible people by deir ac's;

> I'se a-givin' you de Scriptuah,
> I'se a-handin' you de fac's. . . .
> Fu' de Bible says "a servant
> Is a-worthy of his hire."

Here Dunbar moves in and out of dialect almost imperceptibly, between humor and direct finger pointing—all done behind the mask of the Bible. The minister is clever enough to know that someone in the congregation is going to go back and report what happened at the meeting to the master, and that is why he admonishes the congregation:

> Now don't run an' tell yo' mastahs
> Dat I's preachin' discontent.

One must remember how dangerous it must have been to preach about freedom and equality in a time of slavery. So the minister is quick to say

> Dat I'm talkin' 'bout ouah freedom
> In a Bibleistic way.

Dunbar is able to draw laughter from his reader-audience, and maybe it is this trait that causes him most of his troubles.

Dunbar's complex and often ironic linguistic usage can be attributed in part to the society and the times in which he lived. But the pervasive talent behind it exists today in the linguistic skills of contemporary African American youths, specifically spoken word poetry and rap music. Can we in fact, in hindsight, blame Dunbar for his sometimes stereotypical and often ironic uses of dialect without equally examining similar developments in our own time?

In his brief lifetime (1872–1906), less than thirty-four years, Dunbar seems to have been inoculated with the same serum that caused several of the English Romantics to write at such a breakneck speed and then rush headlong into the future. At eighteen or nineteen when Dunbar graduated from high school, the only black in his class, he had a mere fifteen years left to write. In that decade and a half he wrote twelve books of poetry, four novels, four books of short stories, one opera, two musicals, and a variety of one-acts with incidental music. He wrote four full-length plays, three of which are lost and the fourth only recently published for the first time. A number of his wide-ranging essays are yet to be collected. No matter how we perceive his overall output, it was major, and Dunbar was operating under the stress of restrictive times and restricting circumstances.

Writing under conditions the likes of which we can only begin to imagine, Dunbar produced a substantial body of work that is filled with vibrant characters, exhilarating atmosphere, and delightful language. While the poet's later letters evince regret, early in his career Dunbar observed with quiet poignancy, in "The Poet and His Song":

> There are no ears to hear my lays,
> No lips to lift a word of praise;
> But still, with faith unfaltering,
> I live and laugh and love and sing.
> What matters yon unheeding throng?
>   They cannot feel my spirit's spell,
> Since life is sweet and love is long,
>   I sing my song, and all is well.

We are persuaded by the device of humor in numerous Dunbar poems, and we are convinced by the various masks each persona wears. These masks not only obscure the nature of the character, but also serve as poetic devices to obscure the hand of the poet. He suggests in his most famous rondeau, "We Wear the Mask," that the mask is safety; it is protection; it is a defense mechanism for

> We wear the mask that grins and lies,
> It hides our cheeks and shades our eyes,— . . .
> Why should the world be overwise,
> In counting all our tears and sighs?

> Nay, let them only see us, while
>   We wear the mask.

The world of Dunbar's day was not interested in black suffering, and if the truth be told, it may not yet be. The world community may be preoccupied with its own attendant success, and so the poet ends this very formal poem with a prayerlike gesture:

> We smile, but, O great Christ, our cries
> To thee from tortured souls arise.
> We sing, but oh the clay is vile
> Beneath our feet, and long the mile;
> But let the world dream otherwise,
>   We wear the mask!

Dunbar seems to posit his ultimate sense of struggle in this poem. Struggle is for the individual, first, the community, second, and the race, third. Each race struggles to partake of the American Dream Walt Whitman sings about so effectively. In a prophetic way Dunbar wrote a variation on this theme when he penned the rondeau-like poem "He Had His Dream."

> He labored hard and failed at last,
> His sails too weak to bear the blast,
> The raging tempests tore away
> And sent his beating bark astray.
>   But what cared he
>   For wind or sea!
> He said, "The tempest will be short,
> My bark will come to port."
> He saw through every cloud a gleam—
>   He had his dream.

"Dream" is a theme of great importance to African American writers. It was reiterated by Langston Hughes during the Harlem Renaissance, in numerous poems, among them

"Mother to Son" and "A Dream Deferred." This last poem became the signal epigraph for *A Raisin in the Sun*, Lorraine Hansberry's remarkable play about dignity and survival. Thematically, Dream is not a race issue; it is part and parcel of the work of four of our best playwrights: Eugene O'Neill, Arthur Miller, Tennessee Williams, and Edward Albee.

Dunbar is aware of the social and racial climate of his times, and he says as much in an essay entitled "Recession Never." Here is the introductory paragraph:

> It would seem that the man who sits at his desk in the North and writes about the troubles in the South is very apt to be like a doctor who prescribes for a case he has no chance to diagnose. It would be true in this instance, also, if it were not that what has happened in Georgia has happened in Ohio and Illinois. The race riots in North Carolina were a piece with the same proceedings in the state of Lincoln. The men who shoot the Negro in Hogansville are blood brothers to those who hang him in Urbana, and the deed is neither better nor worse because it happens in one section of the country or other. The race spirit in the United States is not local but general. (*The Paul Laurence Dunbar Reader*, p. 36)

Dunbar is in his element when he approaches the theme of racism and lynching, as in "The Haunted Oak." In this poem, the personified tree possesses knowledge of the past, present, and future. So even when the speaker questions himself—

> Pray, why are you so bare, so bare,
>   Oh, bough of the old oak-tree;
> And why, when I go through the shade you throw,
>   Runs a shudder over me?

one already knows the answer. Clearly in this poem Dunbar is not an accommodationist. This poem speaks out against the intimidating and vicious act of lynching. Each stanza is clear and forthright. There is no masking and no disguise.

The same may be said for the poem "The Colored Soldiers," where Dunbar chronicles the act of being inducted into the service of the country during the Civil War:

> So when War, in savage triumph,
>   Spread abroad his funeral pall—
> Then you called the colored soldiers,
>   And they answered to your call.

At some pains to demonstrate the humanity of these colored soldiers, who are willing to pay the ultimate price for the freedom the minister in "An Ante-Bellum Sermon" so espouses, Dunbar writes:

> They were comrades then and brothers,
>   Are they more or less to-day?
> They were good to stop a bullet
>   And to front the fearful fray.
> They were citizens and soldiers,
>   When rebellion raised its head;
> And the traits that made them worthy,—
>   Ah! those virtues are not dead.

So when Dunbar takes up this subject in the essay "Recession Never," we can see his commitment to justice and social equality:

> The new attitude may be interpreted as saying: "Negroes, you may fight for us, but you may not vote for us. You may prove a strong bulwark when the bullets are flying, but you must stand from the line when the ballots are in the air. You may be heroes in war, but you must be cravens in peace."

Dunbar was committed to protesting the injustices and wrongs perpetrated on African Americans of his time. He was also committed to celebrating their valor, their worthiness, and their identifiable humanity in "When Dey 'Listed Colored

Soldiers," a poem that seems to have escaped the eyes of many
of his severest critics. Here we find a subject similar to that of
"The Colored Soldiers." But in this poem the persona knows
the risks of war as well as its expenses. She at once asks the
fiancé-fighter not to enlist in this terrible conflict, but he force-
fully insists. She says:

> Oh, I hugged him, an' I kissed him, an' I baiged him not to go;
> But he tol' me dat his conscience, hit was callin' to him so . . .
> But I t'ought of all de weary miles dat he would have to tramp,
> An' I couldn't be contented w'en dey tuk him to de camp.
> W'y my hea't nigh broke wid grievin' 'twell I seed him on de street;
> Den I felt lak I could go an' th'ow my body at his feet.

There is still something ruminating in her spirit that tells her
war is devastating, and she is more than ever aware of this
when the master and his son go off to fight on the Confederate
side of the Civil War. She desires to soothe the anguish and suf-
fering that her mistresses feel, but she is unaware of how they
will respond because they simply are not able to identify with
what they think of as their servant's untutored thoughts. She
observes:

> An' I didn't know dey feelin's is de ve'y wo'ds dey said
> W'en I tol' 'em I was so'y. Dey had done gin up dey all;
> But dey only seemed mo' proudah dat dey men had hyeahed de call.
> Bofe my mastahs went in gray suits, an' I loved the Yankee blue,
> But I t'ought dat I could sorrer for de losin' of 'em too;
> But I couldn't, for I didn't know de ha'f o' whut I saw,
> 'Twell dey 'listed colo'ed sojers an' my 'Lias went to wah.

None of this deters the speaker in the poem from identifying
with the master's family, she says, noting their tragic and near
tragic ends:

> W'en de women cried an' mou'ned 'em, I could feel it thoo an' thoo,
> For I had a loved un fightin' in de way o' dangah, too.

The tragedy is complete when both the gray and blue lose an important member. But Dunbar is always more than at pains to show the essence of humanity in the African American community.

Because racism kept him from pursuing law as a career, on which he had set his heart in high school, Dunbar was forced to take a job as an elevator operator when no other job was available to him. Still he was industrious. As he took his passengers up and down the elevator, he recited poetry, and took subscriptions for his projected book. William Blocker, a local businessman, financed Dunbar's first book, *Oak and Ivy*, which the poet quickly sold in order to pay his debt to Blocker. Dunbar then proceeded to print and publish *Majors and Minors*, which Howells reviewed.

As we approach the centennial of Dunbar's death it is clear that he was perceptive about voice and the human nature of his characters. His dialect poems are a testament to these attributes. One story concerning Dunbar's abilities has come to me from Judith Anne Still, the daughter of William Grant Still, the dean of African American composers. Her mother, the writer Verna Arvey, recorded in her diary that Still said Richard B. Harrison told him (about 1923) that Dunbar once came to stay at his house and was playing with his child, whom he loved very much. All of a sudden he stood by the mantelpiece and recited the poem that had come into his mind: "Little Brown Baby." He didn't realize how good it was, but Harrison did and begged him to write it down then and there. This was one of those influential relationships that spread in many directions. Richard B. Harrison was not only best man at Dunbar's wedding, but also the principal reason why Dunbar's only full-length play, *Herrick*, survives. Harrison was also the first black actor to play De Lawd in Marc Connelly's *The Green Pastures*.

William Grant Still (1895–1978), twenty-three years Dunbar's junior, studied at Wilberforce University, and used four of Dunbar's poems as epigraphs to his *Symphony No. 1: The Afro-American*. Three of the poems are in dialect and one is in standard English: "Twell de Night Is Pas'," "W'en I Gits Home," "An Ante-Bellum Sermon," and "Ode to Ethiopia." These are signal poems because each one represents one of those essential oral forms indigenous to black American literature: the blues, the spiritual, the sermon, and the traditional lyric.

This classical symphony is infused with Dunbar's talented dialect. In the blues movement there is the longing of the speaker in "Twell de Night Is Pas' ":

> Let the wo'k come ez it will,
> So dat I fin' you, my honey, at las',
> Somewhaih des ovah de hill.

In the second movement Still evokes the essence of the spiritual, which so influenced the culture, when he uses the poem "W'en I Gits Home," where the speaker longs to hear God say: "Enough, Ol' man, come home!" The third movement centers on "The Ante-Bellum Sermon," and the fourth movement captures Dunbar's sense of pride in his heritage in "Ode to Ethiopia," where he writes:

> Be proud, my Race, in mind and soul;
> Thy name is writ on Glory's scroll
>   In characters of fire.
> High 'mid the clouds of Fame's bright sky
> Thy banner's blazoned folds now fly,
>   And truth shall lift them higher.

This sense of black pride appeared in the poetry of Dunbar long before such feelings became fashionable.

Dunbar's influence pervades as well the works of many writers who came after him. Dunbar's legacy can be felt from the poetry of Langston Hughes to the works of the modernist artist Romare Bearden, whose collages are a dialect of traditional shapes and colors. In each case the individual is attempting to make art in a fresh and perceptive way. It is what Dunbar attempted and achieved when he daringly and boldly entered into the world of dialect. In these contemporary times we are likely to praise an author who captures the vernacular in a meaningful and realistic way and satisfies our need to believe what the character is saying. It is high time we "forgave" Paul Laurence Dunbar for practicing his craft and for making—in the process—superb art.

Bibliography

BOOKS BY PAUL LAURENCE DUNBAR

Poetry:

Oak and Ivy. Dayton, Ohio: United Brethren Publishing House, 1893.

Majors and Minors. Toledo, Ohio: Hadley and Hadley, 1895.

Lyrics of Lowly Life. New York: Dodd, Mead and Co., 1896.

Lyrics of the Hearthside. New York: Dodd, Mead and Co., 1899.

Poems of Cabin and Field. New York: Dodd, Mead and Co., 1899.

Candle Lightin' Time. New York: Dodd, Mead and Co., 1901.

Lyrics of Love and Laughter. New York: Dodd, Mead and Co., 1903.

When Malindy Sings. New York: Dodd, Mead and Co., 1903.

Li'l' Gal. New York: Dodd, Mead and Co., 1904.

Lyrics of Sunshine and Shadow. New York: Dodd, Mead and Co., 1904.

Howdy, Honey, Howdy. Toronto: The Musson Book Company, 1905.

Joggin' Erlong. New York: Dodd, Mead and Company, 1906.

The Complete Poems of Paul Laurence Dunbar. New York: Dodd, Mead and Company, 1913.

Lyrics and Texts for Musicals and Operas:

African Romances. Music: Samuel Coleridge Taylor. London: Auginer & Co., 1897.

Clorindy, or The Origin of the Cakewalk. Music: Will Marion Cook. New York: Witmark Music Publishers, 1898.

Dream Lovers. Music: Samuel Coleridge Taylor. London and New York: Boosey & Co., 1898.

In Dahomey. Music: Will Marion Cook. Witmark Music Publishers, 1902.

Short Stories:

Folks from Dixie. New York: Dodd, Mead and Company, 1898.

The Strength of Gideon and Other Stories. New York: Dodd, Mead and Company, 1900.

In Old Plantation Days. New York: Dodd, Mead and Company, 1903.

The Heart of Happy Hollow. New York: Dodd, Mead and Company, 1904.

Novels:

The Uncalled. New York: Dodd, Mead and Company, 1898.

The Love of Landry. New York: Dodd, Mead and Company, 1900.

The Fanatics. New York: Dodd, Mead and Company, 1901.

The Sport of the Gods. New York: Dodd, Mead and Company, 1902.

Suggestions for Further Reading

Alexander, Eleanor. *Lyrics of Sunshine and Shadow: The Tragic Courtship and Marriage of Paul Laurence Dunbar and Alice Ruth Moore*. New York: New York University Press, 2001.

Austin, Charles M. *Paul Laurence Dunbar's Roots and Much More*. Dayton, Ohio: Sense of Roots, 1989.

Brawley, Benjamin. *Paul Laurence Dunbar: Poet of His People*. Chapel Hill: University of North Carolina Press, 1936.

Braxton, Joanne, ed. *The Collected Poems of Paul Laurence Dunbar*. Charlottesville: University Press of Virginia, 1993.

Conover, Charlotte Reeve. *Some Dayton Saints and Prophets*. Dayton; Ohio: United Brethren Publishing House, 1907.

Cunningham, Virginia. *Paul Laurence Dunbar and His Song*. New York: Dodd, Mead and Company, 1947.

Davis, Charles T. *Black Is the Color of the Cosmos: Essays on Black Literature and Culture, 1942—1981*. Edited by Henry Louis Gates, Jr. New York: Garland Publishing, 1982.

Douglass, Frederick. *The Life of Frederick Douglass, an American Slave: Written by Himself*, 1845. Rpt. Garden City, N.Y.: Doubleday and Company, 1963.

Du Bois, W. E. B. *The Souls of Black Folk*. 1903. Rpt. New York: Signet, 1969.

Dunbar, Alice. "The Poet and His Song." *A.M.E. Review* 12 (October 1914): 121–35.

Emanuel, James A. "Racial Fire in the Poetry of Paul Laurence Dunbar." In *A Singer in the Dawn: Reinterpretations of Paul Laurence Dunbar*, edited by Jay Martin, pp. 75–93. New York: Dodd, Mead and Company, 1975.

Fuller, Sara S. *The Paul Laurence Dunbar Collection: An Inventory to the Microfilm Edition*. Columbus: Ohio Historical Society, 1972.

Gates, Henry Louis, Jr. "Dis and Dat: Dialect and the Descent." In

Afro-American Literature: The Reconstruction of Instruction, edited by Robert Stepto and Daxter Fisher, pp. 88–117. New York: Modern Language Association, 1969.

———. *The Signifying Monkey: A Theory of Afro-American Literary Criticism*. New York: Oxford University Press, 1988.

Gayle, Addison, Jr., *Oak and Ivy: A Biography of Paul Laurence Dunbar*. Garden City, N.Y.: Doubleday and Company, 1971.

Gentry, Tony. *Paul Laurence Dunbar*. New York: Chelsea House Publishers, 1989.

Gould, Jean. *That Dunbar Boy*. New York: Dodd, Mead and Company, 1958.

Hayden, Robert. "Paul Laurence Dunbar." In *American Journal*. Taunton, Mass.: Effendi Press, 1978.

Howells, William Dean. Introduction to Paul Laurence Dunbar's *Lyrics of Lowly Life*. New York: Dodd, Mead and Company, 1896.

Hudson, Gossie H. "A Biography of Paul Laurence Dunbar." Ph.D. diss., Ohio State University, 1970.

Hughes, Langston. "Paul Laurence Dunbar, the Robert Burns of Negro Poetry." In *Famous American Negroes*. New York: Dodd, Mead and Company, 1975.

———. "The Negro Artist and the Racial Mountain." *Nation* 122 (June 18, 1926): 692–94.

Hull, Gloria T., ed. *Give Us This Day: The Diary of Alice Dunbar*. New York: W. W. Norton, 1984.

Johnson, James Weldon. *Along This Way*. New York: The Viking Press, 1933.

Kindilien, Carlin T. *American Poetry in the 1890's*. Providence, R.I.: Brown University Press, 1956.

Lawson, Victor. *Dunbar Critically Examined*. Washington, D.C.: The Associated Press, 1941.

Lorde, Audre. *Sister Outsider: Essays and Speeches*. Trumansburg, N.Y.: Crossing Press, 1984.

Lucas, Laryea Doris. "Paul Laurence Dunbar." In *Dictionary of Literary Biography: Afro-American Writers Before the Harlem Renaissance*, ed. by Trudier Harris, vol. 50. Detroit: Book Tower, 1986.

Martin, Herbert Woodward. *Paul Laurence Dunbar: A Singer of Songs*. Columbus: The State Library of Ohio, 1980.

———, and Ronald Primeau. *In His Own Voice: The Dramatic and Other Uncollected Works of Paul Laurence Dunbar*. Athens: Ohio University Press, 2002.

Martin, Jay, ed. *A Singer in the Dawn: Reinterpretations of Paul Laurence Dunbar*. New York: Dodd, Mead and Company, 1975.

——, and Gossie H. Hudson, eds. *The Paul Laurence Dunbar Reader*. New York: Dodd, Mead and Company, 1975.

McKissack, Patricia C. *Paul Laurence Dunbar: A Poet to Remember*. Chicago: Children's Press, 1984.

Metcalf, E. W. *Paul Laurence Dunbar: A Bibliography*. Metuchen, N.J.: Scarecrow Press, 1975.

Nettles, Elsa. *Language, Race, and Social Class in Howells's America*. Lexington: University Press of Kentucky, 1987.

Revell, Peter. *Paul Laurence Dunbar*. Boston: Twayne Publishers, 1979.

Schultz, Pearle H. *Paul Laurence Dunbar: Black Poet Laureate*. Champaign, Ill.: Garrad Publishing Company, 1974.

Turner, Darwin T. "Paul Laurence Dunbar: The Rejected Symbol." *Journal of Negro History* 52 (January 1967): 1–13.

Wagner, Jean. *Black Poets of the United States: From Dunbar to Langston Hughes*. Urbana: University of Illinois Press, 1973.

Wiggins, Lida Keck. *The Life and Works of Paul Laurence Dunbar*. Naperville, Ill.: J. L. Nichols and Company, 1907.

FROM *OAK AND IVY*
1893

A Banjo Song

Oh, dere's lots o' keer an' trouble
   In dis world to swaller down;
An' ol' Sorrer's purty lively
   In her way o' gittin' roun'.
Yet dere's times when I furgit 'em,—
   Aches an' pains an' troubles all,—
An' it's when I tek at ebenin'
   My ol' banjo f'om de wall.

'Bout de time dat night is fallin'
   An' my daily wu'k is done,
An' above de shady hilltops
   I kin see de settin' sun;
When de quiet, restful shadders
   Is beginnin' jes' to fall,—
Den I take de little banjo
   F'om its place upon de wall.

Den my fam'ly gadders roun' me
   In de fadin' o' de light,
Ez I strike de strings to try 'em
   Ef dey all is tuned er-right.
An' it seems we're so nigh heaben
   We kin hyeah de angels sing
When de music o' dat banjo
   Sets my cabin all er-ring.

An' my wife an' all de othahs,—
   Male an' female, small an' big,—
Even up to gray-haired granny,
   Seem jes' boun' to do a jig;
'Twell I change de style o' music,
   Change de movement an' de time,

An' de ringin' little banjo
    Plays an ol' hea't-feelin' hime.

An' somehow my th'oat gits choky,
    An' a lump keeps tryin' to rise
Lak it wan'ed to ketch de water
    Dat was flowin' to my eyes;
An' I feel dat I could sorter
    Knock de socks clean off o' sin
Ez I hyeah my po' ol' granny
    Wif huh tremblin' voice jine in.

Den we all th'ow in our voices
    Fu' to he'p de chune out too,
Lak a big camp-meetin' choiry
    Tryin' to sing a mou'nah th'oo.
An' our th'oahts let out de music,
    Sweet an' solemn, loud an' free,
'Twell de raftahs o' my cabin
    Echo wif de melody.

Oh, de music o' de banjo,
    Quick an' deb'lish, solemn, slow,
Is de greates' joy an' solace
    Dat a weary slave kin know!
So jes' let me hyeah it ringin',
    Dough de chune be po' an' rough,
It's a pleasure; an' de pleasures
    O' dis life is few enough.

Now, de blessed little angels
    Up in heaben, we are told,
Don't do nothin' all dere lifetime
    'Ceptin' play on ha'ps o' gold.
Now I think heaben'd be mo' homelike
    Ef we'd hyeah some music fall
F'om a real ol'-fashioned banjo,
    Like dat one upon de wall.

A Career

"Break me my bounds, and let me fly
To regions vast of boundless sky;
Nor I, like piteous Daphne, be
Root-bound. Ah, no! I would be free
As yon same bird that in its flight
Outstrips the range of mortal sight;
Free as the mountain streams that gush
From bubbling springs, and downward rush
Across the serrate mountain's side,—
The rocks o'erwhelmed, their banks defied,—
And like the passions in the soul,
Swell into torrents as they roll.
Oh, circumscribe me not by rules
That serve to lead the minds of fools!
But give me pow'r to work my will,
And at my deeds the world shall thrill.
My words shall rouse the slumb'ring zest
That hardly stirs in manhood's breast;
And as the sun feeds lesser lights,
As planets have their satellites,
So round about me will I bind
The men who prize a master mind!"

He lived a silent life alone,
And laid him down when it was done;
And at his head was placed a stone
On which was carved a name unknown!

Columbian Ode

I

Four hundred years ago a tangled waste
  Lay sleeping on the west Atlantic's side;
Their devious ways the Old World's millions traced
  Content, and loved, and labored, dared and died,
While students still believed the charts they conned,
  And revelled in their thriftless ignorance,
Nor dreamed of other lands that lay beyond
  Old Ocean's dense, indefinite expanse.

II

But deep within her heart old Nature knew
  That she had once arrayed, at Earth's behest,
Another offspring, fine and fair to view,—
  The chosen suckling of the mother's breast.
The child was wrapped in vestments soft and fine,
  Each fold a work of Nature's matchless art;
The mother looked on it with love divine,
  And strained the loved one closely to her heart.
And there it lay, and with the warmth grew strong
  And hearty, by the salt sea breezes fanned,
Till Time with mellowing touches passed along,
  And changed the infant to a mighty land.

III

But men knew naught of this, till there arose
  That mighty mariner, the Genoese,
Who dared to try, in spite of fears and foes,
  The unknown fortunes of unsounded seas.
O noblest of Italia's sons, thy bark
Went not alone into that shrouding night!
O dauntless darer of the rayless dark,
  The world sailed with thee to eternal light!

The deer-haunts that with game were crowded then
　　To-day are tilled and cultivated lands;
The schoolhouse tow'rs where Bruin had his den,
　　And where the wigwam stood the chapel stands;
The place that nurtured men of savage mien
　　Now teems with men of Nature's noblest types;
Where moved the forest-foliage banner green,
　　Now flutters in the breeze the stars and stripes!

James Whitcomb Riley
(From a Westerner's Point of View.)

No matter what you call it,
　　Whether genius, or art,
He sings the simple songs that come
　　The closest to your heart.
Fur trim an' skillful phrases,
　　I do not keer a jot;
'Tain't the words alone, but feelin's,
　　That tech the tender spot.
An' that's jest why I love him,—
　　Why, he's got sech human feelin',
An' in ev'ry song he gives us,
　　You kin see it creepin', stealin'.
Through the core the tears go tricklin',
　　But the edge is bright an' smiley;
I never saw a poet
　　Like that poet Whitcomb Riley.

His heart keeps beatin' time with our'n
　　In measures fast or slow;
He tells us jest the same ol' things
　　Our souls have learned to know.
He paints our joys an' sorrers
　　In a way so stric'ly true,
That a body can't help knowin'
　　That he has felt them too.

If there's a lesson to be taught,
　　He never fears to teach it,
An' he puts the food so good an' low
　　That the humblest one kin reach it.
Now in our time, when poets rhyme
　　For money, fun, or fashion,
'Tis good to hear one voice so clear
　　That thrills with honest passion.
So let the others build their songs,
　　An' strive to polish highly,—
There's none of them kin tech the heart
　　Like our own Whitcomb Riley.

Life

A crust of bread and a corner to sleep in,
A minute to smile and an hour to weep in,
A pint of joy to a peck of trouble,
And never a laugh but the moans come double;
　　And that is life!

A crust and a corner that love makes precious,
With a smile to warm and the tears to refresh us;
And joy seems sweeter when cares come after,
And a moan is the finest of foils for laughter;
　　And that is life!

Lullaby

Bedtime's come fu' little boys.
     Po' little lamb.
Too tiahed out to make a noise,
     Po' little lamb.
You gwine t' have to-morrer sho'?
Yes, you tole me dat befo',
Don't you fool me, chile, no mo',
     Po' little lamb.

You been bad de livelong day,
     Po' little lamb.
Th'owin' stones an' runnin' 'way,
     Po' little lamb.
My, but you's a-runnin' wil',
Look jes' lak some po' folks chile;
Mam' gwine whup you atter while,
     Po' little lamb.

Come hyeah! you mos' tiahed to def,
     Po' little lamb.
Played yo'se'f clean out o' bref,
     Po' little lamb.
See dem han's now—sich a sight!
Would you evah b'lieve dey's white?
Stan' still twell I wash 'em right,
     Po' little lamb.

Jes' cain't hol' yo' haid up straight,
     Po' little lamb.
Hadn't oughter played so late,
     Po' little lamb.
Mammy do' know whut she'd do,
Ef de chillun's all lak you;

You's a caution now fu' true,
    Po' little lamb.

Lay yo' haid down in my lap,
    Po' little lamb.
Y' ought to have a right good slap,
    Po' little lamb.
You been runnin' roun' a heap.
Shet dem eyes an' don't you peep,
Dah now, dah now, go to sleep,
    Po' little lamb.

Melancholia

Silently without my window,
    Tapping gently at the pane,
    Falls the rain.
Through the trees sighs the breeze
    Like a soul in pain.
Here alone I sit and weep;
Thought hath banished sleep.

Wearily I sit and listen
    To the water's ceaseless drip.
    To my lip
Fate turns up the bitter cup,
    Forcing me to sip;
'Tis a bitter, bitter drink,
Thus I sit and think,—

Thinking things unknown and awful,
    Thoughts on wild, uncanny themes,
    Waking dreams.
Spectres dark, corpses stark,
    Show the gaping seams
Whence the cold and cruel knife
Stole away their life.

Bloodshot eyes all strained and staring,
　Gazing ghastly into mine;
　　Blood like wine
On the brow—clotted now—
　Shows death's dreadful sign.
Lonely vigil still I keep;
Would that I might sleep!

Still, oh, still, my brain is whirling!
　Still runs on my stream of thought;
　　I am caught
In the net fate hath set.
　Mind and soul are brought
To destruction's very brink;
Yet I can but think!

Eyes that look into the future,—
　Peeping forth from out my mind,
　　They will find
Some new weight, soon or late,
　On my soul to bind,
　Crushing all its courage out,—
Heavier than doubt.

Dawn, the Eastern monarch's daughter,
　Rising from her dewy bed,
　　Lays her head
'Gainst the clouds' sombre shrouds
　Now half fringed with red.
O'er the land she 'gins to peep;
Come, O gentle Sleep!

Hark! the morning cock is crowing;
   Dreams, like ghosts, must hie away;
   'Tis the day.
Rosy morn now is born;
   Dark thoughts may not stay.
Day my brain from foes will keep;
Now, my soul, I sleep.

My Sort o' Man

I don't believe in 'ristercrats
   An' never did, you see;
The plain ol' homelike sorter folks
   Is good enough fur me.
O' course, I don't desire a man
   To be too tarnal rough,
But then, I think all folks should know
   When they air nice enough.

Now there is folks in this here world,
   From peasant up to king,
Who want to be so awful nice
   They overdo the thing.
That's jest the thing that makes me sick,
   An' quicker 'n a wink
I set it down that them same folks
   Ain't half so good's you think.

I like to see a man dress nice,
   In clothes becomin' too;
I like to see a woman fix
   As women orter to do;
An' boys an' gals I like to see
   Look fresh an' young an' spry,—
We all must have our vanity
   An' pride before we die.

But I jedge no man by his clothes,—
    Nor gentleman nor tramp;
The man that wears the finest suit
    May be the biggest scamp,
An' he whose limbs air clad in rags
    That make a mournful sight,
In life's great battle may have proved
    A hero in the fight.

I don't believe in 'ristercrats;
    I like the honest tan
That lies upon the healthful cheek
    An' speaks the honest man;
I like to grasp the brawny hand
    That labor's lips have kissed,
For he who has not labored here
    Life's greatest pride has missed:

The pride to feel that yore own strength
    Has cleaved fur you the way
To heights to which you were not born,
    But struggled day by day.
What though the thousands sneer an' scoff,
    An' scorn yore humble birth?
Kings are but puppets; you are king
    By right o' royal worth.

The man who simply sits an' waits
    Fur good to come along,
Ain't worth the breath that one would take
    To tell him he is wrong.
Fur good ain't flowin' round this world
    Fur every fool to sup;
You've got to put yore see-ers on,
    An' go an' hunt it up.

Good goes with honesty, I say,
    To honour an' to bless;

To rich an' poor alike it brings
    A wealth o' happiness.
The 'ristercrats ain't got it all,
    Fur much to their su'prise,
That's one of earth's most blessed things
    They can't monopolize.

Ode to Ethiopia

O Mother Race! to thee I bring
This pledge of faith unwavering,
    This tribute to thy glory.
I know the pangs which thou didst feel,
When Slavery crushed thee with its heel,
    With thy dear blood all gory.

Sad days were those—ah, sad indeed!
But through the land the fruitful seed
    Of better times was growing.
The plant of freedom upward sprung,
And spread its leaves so fresh and young—
    Its blossoms now are blowing.

On every hand in this fair land,
Proud Ethiope's swarthy children stand
    Beside their fairer neighbor;
The forests flee before their stroke,
Their hammers ring, their forges smoke,—
    They stir in honest labour.

They tread the fields where honour calls;
Their voices sound through senate halls
    In majesty and power.
To right they cling; the hymns they sing
Up to the skies in beauty ring,
    And bolder grow each hour.

Be proud, my Race, in mind and soul;
Thy name is writ on Glory's scroll
   In characters of fire.
High 'mid the clouds of Fame's bright sky
Thy banner's blazoned folds now fly,
   And truth shall lift them higher.

Thou hast the right to noble pride,
Whose spotless robes were purified
   By blood's severe baptism.
Upon thy brow the cross was laid,
And labour's painful sweat-beads made
   A consecrating chrism.

No other race, or white or black,
When bound as thou wert, to the rack,
   So seldom stooped to grieving;
No other race, when free again,
Forgot the past and proved them men
   So noble in forgiving.

Go on and up! Our souls and eyes
Shall follow thy continuous rise;
   Our ears shall list thy story
From bards who from thy root shall spring,
And proudly tune their lyres to sing
   Of Ethiopia's glory.

Sympathy

I know what the caged bird feels, alas!
   When the sun is bright on the upland slopes;
When the wind stirs soft through the springing grass,
And the river flows like a stream of glass;
   When the first bird sings and the first bud opes,
And the faint perfume from its chalice steals—
I know what the caged bird feels!

I know why the caged bird beats his wing
   Till its blood is red on the cruel bars;
For he must fly back to his perch and cling
When he fain would be on the bough a-swing;
   And a pain still throbs in the old, old scars
And they pulse again with a keener sting—
I know why he beats his wing!

I know why the caged bird sings, ah me,
   When his wing is bruised and his bosom sore,—
When he beats his bars and he would be free;
It is not a carol of joy or glee,
   But a prayer that he sends from his heart's deep core,
But a plea, that upward to Heaven he flings—
I know why the caged bird sings!

The Ol' Tunes

You kin talk about yer anthems
   An' yer arias an' sich,
An' yer modern choir-singin'
   That you think so awful rich;
But you orter heerd us youngsters
   In the times now far away,
A-singin' o' the ol' tunes
   In the ol'-fashioned way.

There was some of us sung treble
   An' a few of us growled bass,
An' the tide o' song flowed smoothly
   With its 'comp'niment o' grace;
There was spirit in that music,
   An' a kind o' solemn sway,
A-singin' o' the ol' tunes
   In the ol'-fashioned way.

I remember oft o' standin'
  In my homespun pantaloons—
On my face the bronze an' freckle
  O' the suns o' youthful Junes—
Thinkin' that no mortal minstrel
  Ever chanted sich a lay
As the ol' tunes we was singin'
  In the ol'-fashioned way.

The boys 'ud always lead us,
  An' the girls 'ud all chime in
Till the sweetness o' the singin'
  Robbed the list'nin' soul o' sin;
An' I used to tell the parson
  'Twas as good to sing as pray,
When the people sung the ol' tunes
  In the ol'-fashioned way.

How I long ag'in to hear 'em
  Pourin' forth from soul to soul,
With the treble high an' meller,
  An' the bass's mighty roll;
But the times is very diff'rent,
  An' the music heerd to-day
Ain't the singin' o' the ol' tunes
  In the ol'-fashioned way.

Little screechin' by a woman,
  Little squawkin' by a man,
Then the organ's twiddle-twaddle,
  Jest the empty space to span,—
An' ef you should even think it,
  'Tisn't proper fur to say
That you want to hear the ol' tunes
  In the ol'-fashioned way.

But I think that some bright mornin',
   When the toils of life air o'er,
An' the sun o' heaven arisin'
   Glads with light the happy shore,
I shall hear the angel chorus,
   In the realms of endless day,
A-singin' o' the ol' tunes
   In the ol'-fashioned way.

The Seedling

As a quiet little seedling
   Lay within its darksome bed,
To itself it fell a-talking,
   And this is what it said:

"I am not so very robust,
   But I'll do the best I can;"
And the seedling from that moment
   Its work of life began.

So it pushed a little leaflet
   Up into the light of day,
To examine the surroundings
   And show the rest the way.

The leaflet liked the prospect,
   So it called its brother, Stem;
Then two other leaflets heard it,
   And quickly followed them.

To be sure, the haste and hurry
   Made the seedling sweat and pant;
But almost before it knew it
   It found itself a plant.

The sunshine poured upon it,
　　And the clouds they gave a shower;
And the little plant kept growing
　　Till it found itself a flower.

Little folks, be like the seedling,
　　Always do the best you can;
Every child must share life's labor
　　Just as well as every man.

And the sun and showers will help you
　　Through the lonesome, struggling hours,
Till you raise to light and beauty
　　Virtue's fair, unfading flowers.

FROM *MAJORS AND MINORS*
MINORS
1895

After the Quarrel

So we, who've supped the self-same cup,
    To-night must lay our friendship by;
Your wrath has burned your judgment up,
    Hot breath has blown the ashes high.
You say that you are wronged—ah, well,
    I count that friendship poor, at best
A bauble, a mere bagatelle,
    That cannot stand so slight a test.

I fain would still have been your friend,
    And talked and laughed and loved with you;
But since it must, why, let it end;
    The false but dies, 'tis not the true.
So we are favored, you and I,
    Who only want the living truth.
It was not good to nurse the lie;
    'Tis well it died in harmless youth.

I go from you to-night to sleep.
    Why, what's the odds? why should I grieve?
I have no fund of tears to weep
    For happenings that undeceive.
The days shall come, the days shall go
    Just as they came and went before.
The sun shall shine, the streams shall flow
    Though you and I are friends no more.

And in the volume of my years,
    Where all my thoughts and acts shall be,
The page whereon your name appears
    Shall be forever sealed to me.
Not that I hate you over-much,
    'Tis less of hate than love defied;

Howe'er, our hands no more shall touch,
    We'll go our ways, the world is wide.

Alice

Know you, winds that blow your course
    Down the verdant valleys,
That somewhere you must, perforce,
    Kiss the brow of Alice?
When her gentle face you find,
Kiss it softly, naughty wind.

Roses waving fair and sweet
    Thro' the garden alleys,
Grow into a glory meet
    For the eye of Alice;
Let the wind your offering bear
Of sweet perfume, faint and rare.

Lily holding crystal dew
    In your pure white chalice,
Nature kind hath fashioned you
    Like the soul of Alice;
It of purest white is wrought,
Filled with gems of crystal thought.

Ballad

I know my love is true,
    And oh the day is fair.
The sky is clear and blue,
The flowers are rich of hue,
    The air I breathe is rare,
    I have no grief or care;
For my own love is true,
    And oh the day is fair.

My love is false I find,
  And oh the day is dark.
Blows sadly down the wind,
While sorrow holds my mind;
  I do not hear the lark,
  For quenched is life's dear spark,—
My love is false I find,
  And oh the day is dark!

For love doth make the day
  Or dark or doubly bright;
Her beams along the way
Dispel the gloom and gray.
  She lives and all is bright,
  She dies and life is night.
For love doth make the day,
  Or dark or doubly bright.

By the Stream

By the stream I dream in calm delight, and watch as in a glass,
How the clouds like crowds of snowy-hued and white-robed
    maidens pass,
And the water into ripples breaks and sparkles as it spreads,
Like a host of armored knights with silver helmets on their
    heads.
And I deem the stream an emblem fit of human life may go,
For I find a mind may sparkle much and yet but shallows
    show,
And a soul may glow with myriad lights and wondrous mys-
    teries,
When it only lies a dormant thing and mirrors what it sees.

The Change Has Come

The change has come, and Helen sleeps—
Not sleeps; but wakes to greater deeps
Of wisdom, glory, truth, and light,
Than ever blessed her seeking sight,
In this low, long, lethargic night,
    Worn out with strife
    Which men call life.

The change has come, and who would say
"I would it were not come to-day"?
What were the respite till to-morrow?
Postponement of a certain sorrow,
From which each passing day would borrow!
    Let grief be dumb,
    The change has come.

Changing Time

The cloud looked in at the window,
    And said to the day, "Be dark!"
And the roguish rain tapped hard on the pane,
    To stifle the song of the lark.

The wind sprang up in the tree tops
    And shrieked with a voice of death,
But the rough-voiced breeze, that shook the trees,
    Was touched with a violet's breath.

The Colored Soldiers

If the muse were mine to tempt it
    And my feeble voice were strong,
If my tongue were trained to measures,
    I would sing a stirring song.
I would sing a song heroic
    Of those noble sons of Ham,
Of the gallant colored soldiers
    Who fought for Uncle Sam!

In the early days you scorned them,
    And with many a flip and flout
Said "These battles are the white man's,
    And the whites will fight them out."
Up the hills you fought and faltered,
    In the vales you strove and bled,
While your ears still heard the thunder
    Of the foes' advancing tread.

Then distress fell on the nation,
    And the flag was drooping low;
Should the dust pollute your banner?
    No! the nation shouted, No!
So when War, in savage triumph,
    Spread abroad his funeral pall—
Then you called the colored soldiers,
    And they answered to your call.

And like hounds unleashed and eager
    For the life blood of the prey,
Sprung they forth and bore them bravely
    In the thickest of the fray.
And where'er the fight was hottest,
    Where the bullets fastest fell,

There they pressed unblanched and fearless
    At the very mouth of hell.

Ah, they rallied to the standard
    To uphold it by their might;
None were stronger in the labors
    None were braver in the fight.
From the blazing breach of Wagner
    To the plains of Olustee,
They were foremost in the fight
    Of the battles of the free.

And at Pillow! God have mercy
    On the deeds committed there
And the souls of those poor victims
    Sent to Thee without a prayer
Let the fulness of Thy pity
    O'er the hot wrought spirits sway
Of the gallant colored soldiers
    Who fell fighting on that day!

Yes, the Blacks enjoy their freedom,
    And they won it dearly, too;
For the life blood of their thousands
    Did the southern fields bedew.
In the darkness of their bondage,
    In the depths of slavery's night,
Their muskets flashed the dawning,
    And they fought their way to light.

They were comrades then and brothers,
    Are they more or less to-day?
They were good to stop a bullet
    And to front the fearful fray.
They were citizens and soldiers,
    When rebellion raised its head;
And the traits that made them worthy,—
    Ah! those virtues are not dead.

They have shared your nightly vigils,
    They have shared your daily toil;
And their blood with yours commingling
    Has enriched the Southern soil.
They have slept and marched and suffered
    'Neath the same dark skies as you,
They have met as fierce a foeman,
    And have been as brave and true.

And their deeds shall find a record
    In the registry of Fame;
For their blood has cleansed completely
    Every blot of Slavery's shame.
So all honor and all glory
    To those noble sons of Ham—
The gallant colored soldiers
    Who fought for Uncle Sam!

A Corn-Song

On the wide veranda white,
    In the purple failing light,
Sits the master while the sun is lowly burning;
And his dreamy thoughts are drowned
In the softly flowing sound
Of the corn-songs of the field hands slow returning.

    Oh, we hoe de co'n
    Since de ehly mo'n;
    Now de sinkin' sun
    Says de day is done.

O'er the fields with heavy tread,
Light of heart and high of head,
Though the halting steps be labored, slow, and weary;

Still the spirits brave and strong
Find a comforter in song,
And their corn-song rises ever loud and cheery.

> Oh, we hoe de co'n
> Since de ehly mo'n;
> Now de sinkin' sun
> Says de day is done.

To the master in his seat,
Comes the burden, full and sweet,
Of the mellow minor music growing clearer,
As the toilers raise the hymn,
Thro' the silence dusk and dim,
To the cabin's restful shelter drawing nearer.

> Oh, we hoe de co'n
> Since de ehly mo'n;
> Now de sinkin' sun
> Says de day is done.

And a tear is in the eye
Of the master sitting by,
As he listens to the echoes low-replying
To the music's fading calls
As it faints away and falls
Into silence, deep within the cabin dying.

> Oh, we hoe de co'n
> Since de ehly mo'n;
> Now de sinkin' sun
> Says de day is done.

Dawn

An angel, robed in spotless white,
Bent down and kissed the sleeping Night.
Night woke to blush; the sprite was gone.
Men saw the blush and called it Dawn.

Dirge

Place this bunch of mignonette
   In her cold, dead hand;
When the golden sun is set,
   Where the poplars stand,
Bury her from sun and day,
Lay my little love away
     From my sight.

She was like a modest flower
   Blown in sunny June,
Warm as sun at noon's high hour,
   Chaster than the moon.
Ah, her day was brief and bright,
Earth has lost a star of light;
     She is dead.

Softly breathe her name to me,—
   Ah, I loved her so.
Gentle let your tribute be;
   None may better know
Her true worth than I who weep
O'er her as she lies asleep—
     Soft asleep.

Lay these lilies on her breast,
   They are not more white
Than the soul of her, at rest
   'Neath their petals bright.
Chant your aves soft and low,
Solemn be your tread and slow,—
     She is dead.

Lay her here beneath the grass,
   Cool and green and sweet,
Where the gentle brook may pass
   Crooning at her feet.
Nature's bards shall come and sing,
And the fairest flowers shall spring
     Where she lies.

Safe above the water's swirl,
   She has crossed the bar;
Earth has lost a precious pearl,
   Heaven has gained a star,
That shall ever sing and shine,
Till it quells this grief of mine
     For my love.

Disappointed

An old man planted and dug and tended,
   Toiling in joy from dew to dew;
The sun was kind, and the rain befriended;
   Fine grew his orchard and fair to view.
Then he said: "I will quiet my thrifty fears,
For here is fruit for my failing years."

But even then the storm-clouds gathered,
   Swallowing up the azure sky;
The sweeping winds into white foam lathered

The placid breast of the bay, hard by;
Then the spirits that raged in the darkened air
Swept o'er his orchard and left it bare.

The old man stood in the rain, uncaring,
    Viewing the place the storm had swept;
And then with a cry from his soul despairing,
    He bowed him down to the earth and wept.
But a voice cried aloud from the driving rain;
    "Arise, old man, and plant again!"

Ere Sleep Comes Down to Soothe the Weary Eyes

Ere sleep comes down to soothe the weary eyes,
    Which all the day with ceaseless care have sought
The magic gold which from the seeker flies;
    Ere dreams put on the gown and cap of thought,
And make the waking world a world of lies,—
    Of lies most palpable, uncouth, forlorn,
That say life's full of aches and tears and sighs,—
    Oh, how with more than dreams the soul is torn,
Ere sleep comes down to soothe the weary eyes.

Ere sleep comes down to soothe the weary eyes,
    How all the griefs and heartaches we have known
Come up like pois'nous vapors that arise
    From some base witch's caldron, when the crone,
To work some potent spell, her magic plies.
    The past which held its share of bitter pain,
Whose ghost we prayed that Time might exorcise,
    Comes up, is lived and suffered o'er again,
Ere sleep comes down to soothe the weary eyes.

Ere sleep comes down to soothe the weary eyes,
    What phantoms fill the dimly lighted room;
What ghostly shades in awe-creating guise
    Are bodied forth within the teeming gloom.

What echoes faint of sad and soul-sick cries,
   And pangs of vague inexplicable pain
That pay the spirit's ceaseless enterprise,
   Come thronging through the chambers of the brain,
Ere sleep comes down to soothe the weary eyes.

Ere sleep comes down to soothe the weary eyes,
   Where ranges forth the spirit far and free?
Through what strange realms and unfamiliar skies
   Tends her far course to lands of mystery?
To lands unspeakable—beyond surmise,
   Where shapes unknowable to being spring,
Till, faint of wing, the Fancy fails and dies
   Much wearied with the spirit's journeying,
Ere sleep comes down to soothe the weary eyes.

Ere sleep comes down to soothe the weary eyes,
   How questioneth the soul that other soul,—
The inner sense which neither cheats nor lies,
   But self exposes unto self, a scroll
Full writ with all life's acts unwise or wise,
   In characters indelible and known;
So, trembling with the shock of sad surprise,
   The soul doth view its awful self alone,
Ere sleep comes down to soothe the weary eyes.

When sleep comes down to seal the weary eyes,
   The last dear sleep whose soft embrace is balm,
And whom sad sorrow teaches us to prize
   For kissing all our passions into calm,
Ah, then, no more we heed the sad world's cries,
   Or seek to probe th' eternal mystery,
Or fret our souls at long-withheld replies,
   At glooms through which our visions cannot see,
When sleep comes down to seal the weary eyes.

Frederick Douglass

A hush is over all the teeming lists,
    And there is pause, a breath-space in the strife;
A spirit brave has passed beyond the mists
    And vapors that obscure the sun of life.
And Ethiopia, with bosom torn,
Laments the passing of her noblest born.

She weeps for him a mother's burning tears—
    She loved him with a mother's deepest love.
He was her champion thro' direful years,
    And held her weal all other ends above.
When Bondage held her bleeding in the dust,
He raised her up and whispered, "Hope and Trust."

For her his voice, a fearless clarion, rung
    That broke in warning on the ears of men;
For her the strong bow of his power he strung,
    And sent his arrows to the very den
Where grim Oppression held his bloody place
And gloated o'er the mis'ries of a race.

And he was no soft-tongued apologist;
    He spoke straightforward, fearlessly uncowed;
The sunlight of his truth dispelled the mist,
    And set in bold relief each dark hued cloud;
To sin and crime he gave their proper hue,
And hurled at evil what was evil's due.

Through good and ill report he cleaved his way
    Right onward, with his face set toward the heights,
Nor feared to face the foeman's dread array,—

The lash of scorn, the sting of petty spites.
He dared the lightning in the lightning's track,
And answered thunder with his thunder back.

When men maligned him, and their torrent wrath
   In furious imprecations o'er him broke,
He kept his counsel as he kept his path;
   'Twas for his race, not for himself he spoke.
He knew the import of his Master's call,
And felt himself too mighty to be small.

No miser in the good he held was he,—
   His kindness followed his horizon's rim.
His heart, his talents, and his hands were free
   To all who truly needed aught of him.
Where poverty and ignorance were rife,
He gave his bounty as he gave his life.

The place and cause that first aroused his might
   Still proved its power until his latest day.
In Freedom's lists and for the aid of Right
   Still in the foremost rank he waged the fray;
Wrong lived; his occupation was not gone.
He died in action with his armor on!

We weep for him, but we have touched his hand,
   And felt the magic of his presence nigh,
The current that he sent throughout the land,
   The kindling spirit of his battle-cry.
O'er all that holds us we shall triumph yet,
And place our banner where his hopes were set!

Oh, Douglass, thou hast passed beyond the shore,
   But still thy voice is ringing o'er the gale!
Thou'st taught thy race how high her hopes may soar,
   And bade her seek the heights, nor faint, nor fail.
She will not fail, she heeds thy stirring cry,

She knows thy guardian spirit will be nigh,
And, rising from beneath the chast'ning rod,
She stretches out her bleeding hands to God!

A Frolic

Swing yo' lady roun' an' roun',
   Do de bes' you know;
Mek yo' bow an' p'omenade
   Up an' down de flo';
Mek dat banjo hump huhse'f,
   Listen at huh talk:
Mastah gone to town to-night;
   'Tain't no time to walk.

Lif' yo' feet an' flutter thoo,
   Run, Miss Lucy, run;
Reckon you'll be cotched an' kissed
   'Fo' de night is done.
You don't need to be so proud—
   I's a-watchin' you,
An' I's layin' lots o' plans
   Fu' to git you, too.

Moonlight on de cotton-fiel'
   Shinin' sof' an' white,
Whippo'will a-tellin' tales
   Out thaih in de night;
An' yo' cabin's 'crost de lot:
   Run, Miss Lucy, run;
Reckon you'll be cotched an' kissed
   'Fo' de night is done.

He Had His Dream

He had his dream, and all through life,
Worked up to it through toil and strife.
Afloat fore'er before his eyes,
It colored for him all his skies:
    The storm-cloud dark
    Above his bark,
The calm and listless vault of blue
Took on its hopeful hue,
It tinctured every passing beam—
    He had his dream.

He labored hard and failed at last,
His sails too weak to bear the blast,
The raging tempests tore away
And sent his beating bark astray.
    But what cared he
    For wind or sea!
He said, "The tempest will be short,
My bark will come to port."
He saw through every cloud a gleam—
    He had his dream.

Hymn

O li'l' lamb out in de col',
De Mastah call you to de fol',
    O li'l' lamb!
He hyeah you bleatin' on de hill;
Come hyeah an' keep yo' mou'nin' still,
    O li'l' lamb!

De Mastah sen' de Shepud fo'f;
He wandah souf, he wandah no'f,
    O li'l' lamb!
He wandah eas', he wandah wes';
De win' a-wrenchin' at his breas',
    O li'l' lamb!

Oh, tell de Shepud whaih you hide;
He want you walkin' by his side,
    O li'l' lamb!
He know you weak, he know you so';
But come, don' stay away no mo',
    O li'l' lamb!

An' af'ah while de lamb he hyeah
De Shepud's voice a-callin' cleah—
    Sweet li'l' lamb!
He answah f'om de brambles thick,
"O Shepud, I's a-comin' quick"—
    O li'l' lamb!

Invitation to Love

Come when the nights are bright with stars
    Or when the moon is mellow;
Come when the sun his golden bars
    Drops on the hay-field yellow.
Come in the twilight soft and gray,
Come in the night or come in the day,
Come, O love, whene'er you may,
    And you are welcome, welcome.

You are sweet, O Love, dear Love,
You are soft as the nesting dove.
Come to my heart and bring it rest
As the bird flies home to its welcome nest.

Come when my heart is full of grief
   Or when my heart is merry;
Come with the falling of the leaf
   Or with the redd'ning cherry.
Come when the year's first blossom blows,
Come when the summer gleams and glows,
Come with the winter's drifting snows,
   And you are welcome, welcome.

Ione

I

Ah, yes, 'tis sweet still to remember,
   Though 'twere less painful to forget;
For while my heart glows like an ember,
   Mine eyes with sorrow's drops are wet,
   And, oh, my heart is aching yet.
It is a law of mortal pain
   That old wounds, long accounted well,
   Beneath the memory's potent spell,
Will wake to life and bleed again.

So 'tis with me; it might be better
   If I should turn no look behind,—
If I could curb my heart, and fetter
   From reminiscent gaze my mind,
   Or let my soul go blind—go blind!
But would I do it if I could?
   Nay! ease at such a price were spurned;
   For, since my love was once returned,
All that I suffer seemeth good.

I know, I know it is the fashion,
   When love has left some heart distressed,
To weight the air with wordful passion;
   But I am glad that in my breast
   I ever held so dear a guest.

Love does not come at every nod,
  Or every voice that calleth "hasten;"
  He seeketh out some heart to chasten,
And whips it, wailing, up to God!

Love is no random road wayfarer
  Who where he may must sip his glass.
Love is the King, the Purple-Wearer,
  Whose guard recks not of tree or grass
  To blaze the way that he may pass.
What if my heart be in the blast
  That heralds his triumphant way;
  Shall I repine, shall I not say:
"Rejoice, my heart, the King has passed!"

In life, each heart holds some sad story—
  The saddest ones are never told.
I, too, have dreamed of fame and glory,
  And viewed the future bright with gold;
  But that is as a tale long told.
Mine eyes have lost their youthful flash,
  My cunning hand has lost its art;
  I am not old, but in my heart
The ember lies beneath the ash.

I loved! Why not? My heart was youthful,
  My mind was filled with healthy thought.
He doubts not whose own self is truthful,
  Doubt by dishonesty is taught;
  So loved I boldly, fearing naught.
I did not walk this lowly earth;
  Mine was a newer, higher sphere,
  Where youth was long and life was dear,
And all save love was little worth.

Her likeness! Would that I might limn it,
  As Love did, with enduring art;
Nor dust of days nor death may dim it,

Where it lies graven on my heart,
Of this sad fabric of my life a part.
I would that I might paint her now
   As I beheld her in that day,
   Ere her first bloom had passed away,
And left the lines upon her brow.

A face serene that, beaming brightly,
   Disarmed the hot sun's glances bold.
A foot that kissed the ground so lightly,
   He frowned in wrath and deemed her cold,
   But loved her still though he was old.
A form where every maiden grace
   Bloomed to perfection's richest flower,—
   The statued pose of conscious power,
Like lithe-limbed Dian's of the chase.

Beneath a brow too fair for frowning,
   Like moon-lit deeps that glass the skies
Till all the hosts above seem drowning,
   Looked forth her steadfast hazel eyes,
   With gaze serene and purely wise.
And over all, her tresses rare,
   Which, when, with his desire grown weak,
   The Night bent down to kiss her cheek,
Entrapped and held him captive there.

This was Ione; a spirit finer
   Ne'er burned to ash its house of clay;
A soul instinct with fire diviner
   Ne'er fled athwart the face of day,
   And tempted Time with earthly stay.
Her loveliness was not alone
   Of face and form and tresses' hue;
   For aye a pure, high soul shone through
Her every act: this was Ione.

II

'Twas in the radiant summer weather,
  When God looked, smiling, from the sky;
And we went wand'ring much together
  By wood and lane, Ione and I,
  Attracted by the subtle tie
Of common thoughts and common tastes,
  Of eyes whose vision saw the same,
  And freely granted beauty's claim
Where others found but worthless wastes.

We paused to hear the far bells ringing
  Across the distance, sweet and clear.
We listened to the wild bird's singing
  The song he meant for his mate's ear,
  And deemed our chance to do so dear.
We loved to watch the warrior Sun,
  With flaming shield and flaunting crest,
  Go striding down the gory West,
When Day's long fight was fought and won.

And life became a different story;
  Where'er I looked, I saw new light.
Earth's self assumed a greater glory,
  Mine eyes were cleared to fuller sight.
  Then first I saw the need and might
Of that fair band, the singing throng,
  Who, gifted with the skill divine,
  Take up the threads of life, spun fine,
And weave them into soulful song.

They sung for me, whose passion pressing
  My soul, found vent in song nor line.
They bore the burden of expressing
  All that I felt, with art's design,
  And every word of theirs was mine.

I read them to Ione, ofttimes,
  By hill and shore, beneath fair skies,
  And she looked deeply in mine eyes,
And knew my love spoke through their rhymes.

Her life was like the stream that floweth,
  And mine was like the waiting sea;
Her love was like the flower that bloweth,
  And mine was like the searching bee—
  I found her sweetness all for me.
God plied him in the mint of time,
  And coined for us a golden day,
  And rolled it ringing down life's way
With love's sweet music in its chime.

And God unclasped the Book of Ages,
  And laid it open to our sight;
Upon the dimness of its pages,
  So long consigned to rayless night,
  He shed the glory of his light.
We read them well, we read them long,
  And ever thrilling did we see
  That love ruled all humanity,—
The master passion, pure and strong.

III

To-day my skies are bare and ashen,
  And bend on me without a beam.
Since love is held the master-passion,
  Its loss must be the pain supreme—
And grinning Fate has wrecked my dream.
But pardon, dear departed Guest,
  I will not rant, I will not rail;
  For good the grain must feel the flail;
There are whom love has never blessed.

I had and have a younger brother,
    One whom I loved and love to-day
As never fond and doting mother
    Adored the babe who found its way
    From heavenly scenes into her day.
Oh, he was full of youth's new wine,—
    A man on life's ascending slope,
    Flushed with ambition, full of hope;
And every wish of his was mine.

A kingly youth; the way before him
    Was thronged with victories to be won;
So joyous, too, the heavens o'er him
    Were bright with an unchanging sun,—
    His days with rhyme were overrun.
Toil had not taught him Nature's prose,
    Tears had not dimmed his brilliant eyes,
    And sorrow had not made him wise;
His life was in the budding rose.

I know not how I came to waken,
    Some instinct pricked my soul to sight;
My heart by some vague thrill was shaken,—
    A thrill so true and yet so slight,
    I hardly deemed I read aright.
As when a sleeper, ign'rant why,
    Not knowing what mysterious hand
    Has called him out of slumberland,
Starts up to find some danger nigh.

Love is a guest that comes, unbidden,
    But, having come, asserts his right;
He will not be repressed nor hidden.
    And so my brother's dawning plight
    Became uncovered to my sight.

Some sound-mote in his passing tone
   Caught in the meshes of my ear;
   Some little glance, a shade too dear,
Betrayed the love he bore Ione.

What could I do? He was my brother,
   And young, and full of hope and trust;
I could not, dared not try to smother
   His flame, and turn his heart to dust.
   I knew how oft life gives a crust
To starving men who cry for bread;
   But he was young, so few his days,
   He had not learned the great world's ways,
Nor Disappointment's volumes read.

However fair and rich the booty,
   I could not make his loss my gain.
For love is dear, but dearer duty,
   I saw how I could save him pain.
And so, with all my day grown dim,
   That this loved brother's sun might shine,
   I joined his suit, gave over mine,
And sought Ione, to plead for him.

I found her in an eastern bower,
   Where all day long the am'rous sun
Lay by to woo a timid flower.
   This day his course was well-nigh run,
   But still with lingering art he spun
Gold fancies on the shadowed wall.
   The vines waved soft and green above,
   And there where one might tell his love,
I told my griefs—I told her all!

I told her all, and as she hearkened,
   A tear-drop fell upon her dress.
With grief her flushing brow was darkened;
   One sob that she could not repress

Betrayed the depths of her distress.
Upon her grief my sorrow fed,
 And I was bowed with unlived years,
 My heart swelled with a sea of tears,
The tears my manhood could not shed.

The world is Rome, and Fate is Nero,
 Disporting in the hour of doom.
God made us men; times make the hero—
 But in that awful space of gloom
 I gave no thought but sorrow's room.
All—all was dim within that bower,
 What time the sun divorced the day;
 And all the shadows, glooming gray,
Proclaimed the sadness of the hour.

She could not speak—no word was needed;
 Her look, half strength and half despair,
Told me I had not vainly pleaded,
 That she would not ignore my prayer.
 And so she turned and left me there,
And as she went, so passed my bliss;
 She loved me, I could not mistake—
 But for her own and my love's sake,
Her womanhood could rise to this!

My wounded heart fled swift to cover,
 And life at times seemed very drear.
My brother proved an ardent lover—
 What had so young a man to fear?
 He wed Ione within the year.
No shadow clouds her tranquil brow,
 Men speak her husband's name with pride,
 While she sits honored at his side—
She is—she must be happy now!

I doubt the course I took no longer,
   Since those I love seem satisfied.
The bond between them will grow stronger
   As they go forward side by side;
   Then will my pains be justified.
Their joy is mine, and that is best—
   I am not totally bereft;
   For I have still the mem'ry left—
Love stopped with me—a Royal Guest!

The Master-Player

An old, worn harp that had been played
Till all its strings were loose and frayed,
Joy, Hate, and Fear, each one essayed,
To play. But each in turn had found
No sweet responsiveness of sound.

Then Love the Master-Player came
With heaving breast and eyes aflame;
The Harp he took all undismayed,
Smote on its strings, still strange to song,
And brought forth music sweet and strong.

Ode for Memorial Day

Done are the toils and the wearisome marches,
   Done is the summons of bugle and drum.
Softly and sweetly the sky overarches,
   Shelt'ring a land where Rebellion is dumb.
Dark were the days of the country's derangement,
   Sad were the hours when the conflict was on,
But through the gloom of fraternal estrangement
   God sent his light, and we welcome the dawn.

O'er the expanse of our mighty dominions,
    Sweeping away to the uttermost parts,
Peace, the wide-flying, on untiring pinions,
    Bringeth her message of joy to our hearts.

Ah, but this joy which our minds cannot measure,
    What did it cost for our fathers to gain!
Bought at the price of the heart's dearest treasure,
    Born out of travail and sorrow and pain;
Born in the battle where fleet Death was flying,
    Slaying with sabre-stroke bloody and fell;
Born where the heroes and martyrs were dying,
    Torn by the fury of bullet and shell.
Ah, but the day is past: silent the rattle,
    And the confusion that followed the fight.
Peace to the heroes who died in the battle,
    Martyrs to truth and the crowning of Right!

Out of the blood of a conflict fraternal,
    Out of the dust and the dimness of death,
Burst into blossoms of glory eternal
    Flowers that sweeten the world with their breath.
Flowers of charity, peace, and devotion
    Bloom in the hearts that are empty of strife;
Love that is boundless and broad as the ocean
    Leaps into beauty and fulness of life.
So, with the singing of pæans and chorals,
    And with the flag flashing high in the sun,
Place on the graves of our heroes the laurels
    Which their unfaltering valor has won!

One Life

Oh, I am hurt to death, my Love;
    The shafts of Fate have pierced my striving heart,
And I am sick and weary of

The endless pain and smart.
My soul is weary of the strife,
And chafes at life, and chafes at life.

Time mocks me with fair promises;
    A blooming future grows a barren past,
Like rain my fair full-blossomed trees
    Unburden in the blast.
The harvest fails on grain and tree,
Nor comes to me, nor comes to me.

The stream that bears my hopes abreast
    Turns ever from my way its pregnant tide.
My laden boat, torn from its rest,
    Drifts to the other side.
So all my hopes are set astray,
And drift away, and drift away.

The lark sings to me at the morn,
    And near me wings her skyward-soaring flight;
But pleasure dies as soon as born,
    The owl takes up the night,
And night seems long and doubly dark;
I miss the lark, I miss the lark.

Let others labor as they may,
    I'll sing and sigh alone, and write my line.
Their fate is theirs, or grave or gay,
    And mine shall still be mine.
I know the world holds joy and glee,
But not for me,—'tis not for me.

The Poet and His Song

A song is but a little thing,
And yet what joy it is to sing!
In hours of toil it gives me zest,

And when at eve I long for rest;
When cows come home along the bars,
    And in the fold I hear the bell,
As Night, the shepherd, herds his stars,
    I sing my song, and all is well.

There are no ears to hear my lays,
No lips to lift a word of praise;
But still, with faith unfaltering,
I live and laugh and love and sing.
What matters yon unheeding throng?
    They cannot feel my spirit's spell,
Since life is sweet and love is long,
    I sing my song, and all is well.

My days are never days of ease;
I till my ground and prune my trees.
When ripened gold is all the plain,
I put my sickle to the grain.
I labor hard, and toil and sweat,
    While others dream within the dell;
But even while my brow is wet,
    I sing my song, and all is well.

Sometimes the sun, unkindly hot,
My garden makes a desert spot;
Sometimes a blight upon the tree
Takes all my fruit away from me;
And then with throes of bitter pain
    Rebellious passions rise and swell;
But—life is more than fruit or grain,
    And so I sing, and all is well.

A Prayer

O Lord, the hard-won miles
    Have worn my stumbling feet:
Oh, soothe me with thy smiles,
    And make my life complete.

The thorns were thick and keen
    Where'er I trembling trod;
The way was long between
    My wounded feet and God.

Where healing waters flow
    Do thou my footsteps lead.
My heart is aching so;
    Thy gracious balm I need.

Retort

"Thou art a fool," said my head to my heart,
"Indeed, the greatest of fools thou art,
    To be led astray by the trick of a tress,
By a smiling face or a ribbon smart;"
    And my heart was in sore distress.

Then Phyllis came by, and her face was fair,
The light gleamed soft on her raven hair;
    And her lips were blooming a rosy red.
Then my heart spoke out with a right bold air:
    "Thou art worse than a fool, O head!"

Ships That Pass in the Night

Out in the sky the great dark clouds are massing;
    I look far out into the pregnant night,
Where I can hear a solemn booming gun
    And catch the gleaming of a random light,
That tells me that the ship I seek is passing, passing.

My tearful eyes my soul's deep hurt are glassing;
    For I would hail and check that ship of ships.
I stretch my hands imploring, cry aloud,
    My voice falls dead a foot from mine own lips,
And but its ghost doth reach that vessel, passing, passing.

O Earth, O Sky, O Ocean, both surpassing,
    O heart of mine, O soul that dreads the dark!
Is there no hope for me? Is there no way
    That I may sight and check that speeding bark
Which out of sight and sound is passing, passing?

A Summer's Night

The night is dewy as a maiden's mouth,
    The skies are bright as are a maiden's eyes,
    Soft as a maiden's breath the wind that flies
Up from the perfumed bosom of the South.
Like sentinels, the pines stand in the park;
    And hither hastening, like rakes that roam,
    With lamps to light their wayward footsteps home,
The fireflies come stagg'ring down the dark.

We Wear the Mask

We wear the mask that grins and lies,
It hides our cheeks and shades our eyes,—
This debt we pay to human guile;
With torn and bleeding hearts we smile,
And mouth with myriad subtleties.

Why should the world be overwise,
In counting all our tears and sighs?
Nay, let them only see us, while
    We wear the mask.

We smile, but, O great Christ, our cries
To thee from tortured souls arise.
We sing, but oh the clay is vile
Beneath our feet, and long the mile;
But let the world dream otherwise,
    We wear the mask!

To Pfrimmer
(Lines on reading Driftwood.)

Driftwood gathered here and there
Along the beach of time;
Now and then a chip of truth
'Mid boards and boughs of rhyme;
Driftwood gathered day by day,—
The cypress and the oak,—
Twigs that in some former time
From sturdy home trees broke.

Did this wood come floating thick
All along down "Injin Crik?"
Or did kind tides bring it thee
From the past's receding sea
Down the stream of memory?

FROM *LYRICS OF LOWLY LIFE*
1896

Accountability

Folks ain't got no right to censuah othah folks about dey
    habits;
Him dat giv' de squir'ls de bushtails made de bobtails fu' de
    rabbits.
Him dat built de gread big mountains hollered out de little
    valleys,
Him dat made de streets an' driveways wasn't shamed to
    make de alleys.

We is all constructed diff'ent, d'ain't no two of us de same;
We cain't he'p ouah likes an' dislikes, ef we'se bad we ain't to
    blame.
Ef we'se good, we needn't show off, case you bet it ain't ouah
    doin'
We gits into su'ttain channels dat we jes' cain't he'p pu'suin'.

But we all fits into places dat no othah ones could fill,
An' we does the things we has to, big er little, good er ill.
John cain't tek de place o' Henry, Su an' Sally ain't alike;
Bass ain't nuthin' like a suckah, chub ain't nuthin' like a pike.

When you come to think about it, how it's all planned out it's
    splendid.
Nuthin's done er evah happens, 'doubt hit's somefin' dat's
    intended;
Don't keer whut you does, you has to, an' hit sholy beats de
    dickens,—
Viney, go put on de kittle, I got one o' mastah's chickens.

An Ante-Bellum Sermon

We is gathahed hyeah, my brothahs,
  In dis howlin' wildaness,
Fu' to speak some words of comfo't
  To each othah in distress.
An' we chooses fu' ouah subjic'
  Dis—we'll 'splain it by an' by;
  "An' de Lawd said, 'Moses, Moses,'
  An' de man said, 'Hyeah am I.' "

Now ole Pher'oh, down in Egypt,
  Was de wuss man evah bo'n,
An' he had de Hebrew chillun
  Down dah wukin' in his co'n;
'T well de Lawd got tiahed o' his foolin',
  An' sez he: "I'll let him know—
Look hyeah, Moses, go tell Pher'oh
  Fu' to let dem chillun go."

"An' ef he refuse to do it,
  I will make him rue de houah,
Fu' I'll empty down on Egypt
  All de vials of my powah."
Yes, he did—an' Pher'oh's ahmy
  Wasn't wuth a ha'f a dime;
Fu' de Lawd will he'p his chillun,
  You kin trust him evah time.

An' yo' enemies may 'sail you
  In de back an' in de front;
But de Lawd is all aroun' you,
  Fu' to ba' de battle's brunt.
Dey kin fo'ge yo' chains an' shackles

F'om de mountains to de sea;
But de Lawd will sen' some Moses
    Fu' to set his chillun free.

An de lan' shall hyeah his thundah,
    Lak a blas' f'om Gab'el's ho'n,
Fu' de Lawd of hosts is mighty
    When he girds his ahmor on.
But fu' feah some one mistakes me,
    I will pause right hyeah to say,
Dat I'm still a-preachin' ancient,
    I ain't talkin' 'bout to-day.

But I tell you, fellah christuns,
    Things'll happen mighty strange;
Now, de Lawd done dis fu' Isrul,
    An' his ways don't nevah change,
An' de love he showed to Isrul
    Wasn't all on Isrul spent;
Now don't run an' tell yo' mastahs
    Dat I's preachin' discontent.

'Cause I isn't; I'se a-judgin'
    Bible people by deir ac's;
I'se a-givin' you de Scriptuah,
    I'se a-handin' you de fac's.
Cose ole Pher'oh b'lieved in slav'ry,
    But de Lawd he let him see,
Dat de people he put bref in,—
    Evah mothah's son was free.

An' dahs othahs thinks lak Pher'oh,
    But dey calls de Scriptuah liar,
Fu' de Bible says "a servant
    Is a-worthy of his hire."
An' you cain't git roun' nor thoo dat,

An' you cain't git ovah it,
Fu' whatevah place you git in,
   Dis hyeah Bible too 'll fit.

So you see de Lawd's intention,
   Evah sence de worl' began,
Was dat His almighty freedom
   Should belong to evah man,
But I think it would be bettah,
   Ef I'd pause agin to say,
Dat I'm talkin' 'bout ouah freedom
   In a Bibleistic way.

But de Moses is a-comin',
   An' he's comin', suah and fas'
We kin hyeah his feet a-trompin',
   We kin hyeah his trumpit blas'.
But I want to wa'n you people,
   Don't you git too brigity;
An' don't you git to braggin'
   'Bout dese things, you wait an' see.

But when Moses wif his powah
   Comes an' sets us chillun free,
We will praise de gracious Mastah
   Dat has gin us liberty;
An' we'll shout ouah halleluyahs,
   On dat mighty reck'nin' day,
When we'se reco'nised ez citiz'—
   Huh uh! Chillun, let us pray!

The Corn-Stalk Fiddle

When the corn's all cut and the bright stalks shine
   Like the burnished spears of a field of gold;
When the field-mice rich on the nubbins dine,

And the frost comes white and the wind blows cold;
Then it's heigho! fellows and hi-diddle-diddle,
For the time is ripe for the corn-stalk fiddle.

And you take a stalk that is straight and long,
    With an expert eye to its worthy points,
And you think of the bubbling strains of song
    That are bound between its pithy joints—
Then you cut out strings, with a bridge in the middle,
With a corn-stalk bow for a corn-stalk fiddle.

Then the strains that grow as you draw the bow
    O'er the yielding strings with a practised hand!
And the music's flow never loud but low
    Is the concert note of a fairy band.
Oh, your dainty songs are a misty riddle
To the simple sweets of the corn-stalk fiddle.

When the eve comes on, and our work is done,
    And the sun drops down with a tender glance,
With their hearts all prime for the harmless fun,
    Come the neighbor girls for the evening's dance,
And they wait for the well-known twist and twiddle—
More time than tune—from the corn-stalk fiddle.

Then brother Jabez takes the bow,
    While Ned stands off with Susan Bland,
Then Henry stops by Milly Snow,
    And John takes Nellie Jones's hand,
While I pair off with Mandy Biddle,
And scrape, scrape, scrape goes the corn-stalk fiddle.

"Salute your partners," comes the call,
    "All join hands and circle round,"
"Grand train back," and "Balance all,"
    Footsteps lightly spurn the ground.
"Take your lady and balance down the middle"
To the merry strains of the corn-stalk fiddle.

So the night goes on and the dance is o'er,
    And the merry girls are homeward gone,
But I see it all in my sleep once more,
    And I dream till the very break of dawn
Of an impish dance on a red-hot griddle
To the screech and scrape of a corn-stalk fiddle.

The Lawyers' Ways

I've been list'nin' to them lawyers
    In the court house up the street,
An' I've come to the conclusion
    That I'm most completely beat.
Fust one feller riz to argy,
    An' he boldly waded in
As he dressed the tremblin' pris'ner
    In a coat o' deep-dyed sin.

Why, he painted him all over
    In a hue o' blackest crime,
An' he smeared his reputation
    With the thickest kind o' grime,
Tell I found myself a-wond'rin',
    In a misty way and dim,
How the Lord had come to fashion
    Sich an awful man as him.

Then the other lawyer started,
    An' with brimmin', tearful eyes,
Said his client was a martyr
    That was brought to sacrifice.
An' he give to that same pris'ner
    Every blessed human grace,
Tell I saw the light o' virtue
    Fairly shinin' from his face.

Then I own 'at I was puzzled
　　How sich things could rightly be;
An' this aggervatin' question
　　Seems to keep a-puzzlin' me.
So, will some one please inform me,
　　An' this mystery unroll—
How an angel an' a devil
　　Can persess the self-same soul?

Religion

I am no priest of crooks nor creeds,
For human wants and human needs
Are more to me than prophets' deeds;
And human tears and human cares
Affect me more than human prayers.

Go, cease your wail, lugubrious saint!
You fret high Heaven with your plaint.
Is this the "Christian's joy" you paint?
Is this the Christian's boasted bliss?
Avails your faith no more than this?

Take up your arms, come out with me,
Let Heav'n alone; humanity
Needs more and Heaven less from thee.
With pity for mankind look 'round;
Help them to rise—and Heaven is found.

After a Visit

I be'n down in ole Kentucky
　　Fur a week er two, an' say,
'Twuz ez hard ez breakin' oxen
　　Fur to tear myse'f away.
Allus argerin' 'bout fren'ship

An' yer hospitality—
Y' ain't no right to talk about it
Tell you be'n down there to see.

See jest how they give you welcome
    To the best that's in the land,
Feel the sort o' grip they give you
    When they take you by the hand.
Hear 'em say, "We're glad to have you,
    Better stay a week er two;"
An' the way they treat you makes you
    Feel that ev'ry word is true.

Feed you tell you hear the buttons
    Crackin' on yore Sunday vest;
Haul you roun' to see the wonders
    Tell you have to cry for rest.
Drink yer health an' pet an' praise you
    Tell you git to feel ez great
Ez the Sheriff o' the county
    Er the Gov'ner o' the State.

Wife, she sez I must be crazy
    'Cause I go on so, an' Nelse
He 'lows, "Goodness gracious! daddy,
    Cain't you talk about nuthin' else?"
Well, pleg-gone it, I'm jes' tickled,
    Bein' tickled ain't no sin;
I be'n down in ole Kentucky,
    An' I want o' go ag'in.

The Spellin'-Bee

I never shall furgit that night when father hitched up Dobbin,
An' all us youngsters clambered in an' down the road went
    bobbin'

Fur, la! he'd learned a thing er two an' made his blessin'
        shorter.
'Twas late an' cold when we got out, but Nettie liked cold
        weather,
An' so did I, so we agreed we'd jest walk home together.
We both wuz silent, fur of words we nuther had a surplus,
'Till she spoke out quite sudden like, "You missed that word
        on purpose."
Well, I declare it frightened me; at first I tried denyin',
But Nettie, she jest smiled an' smiled, she knowed that I was
        lyin'.
Sez she: "That book is yourn by right;" sez I: "It never could
        be—
I—I—you—ah—" an' there I stuck, an' well she understood
        me.
So we agreed that later on when age had giv' us tether,
We'd jine our lots an' settle down to own that book together.

Keep A-Pluggin' Away

I've a humble little motto
That is homely, though it's true,—
    Keep a-pluggin' away.
It's a thing when I've an object
That I always try to do,—
    Keep a-pluggin' away.
When you've rising storms to quell,
When opposing waters swell,
It will never fail to tell,—
    Keep a-pluggin' away.

If the hills are high before
And the paths are hard to climb,
    Keep a-pluggin' away.
And remember that successes
Come to him who bides his time,—
    Keep a-pluggin' away.

To school where we was kep' at work in every kind o'
        weather,
But where that night a spellin'-bee was callin' us together.
'Twas one o' Heaven's banner nights, the stars was all a-glitter,
The moon was shinin' like the hand o' God had jest then lit
        her.
The ground was white with spotless snow, the blast was sort
        o' stingin';
But underneath our round-abouts, you bet our hearts was
        singin'.
That spellin'-bee had be'n the talk o' many a precious mo-
        ment,
The youngsters all was wild to see jes' what the precious show
        meant,
An' we whose years was in their teens was little less desirous
O' gittin' to the meetin' so's our sweethearts could admire us.
So on we went so anxious fur to satisfy our mission
That father had to box our ears, to smother our ambition.
But boxin' ears was too short work to hinder our arrivin',
He jest turned roun' an' smacked us all, an' kep' right on
        a-drivin'.
Well, soon the schoolhouse hove in sight, the winders beamin'
        brightly;
The sound o' talkin' reached our ears, and voices laffin'
        lightly.
It puffed us up so full an' big 'at I'll jest bet a dollar,
There wa'n't a feller there but felt the strain upon his collar.
So down we jumped an' in we went ez sprightly ez you make
        'em,
But somethin' grabbed us by the knees an' straight began to
        shake 'em.
Fur once within that lighted room, our feelin's took a canter,
An' scurried to the zero mark ez quick ez Tam O'Shanter.
'Cause there was crowds o' people there, both sexes an' all
        stations;
It looked like all the town had come an' brought all their
        relations.
The first I saw was Nettie Gray, I thought that girl was dearer

'N' gold; an' when I got a chance, you bet I aidged up near
    her.
An' Farmer Dobbs's girl was there, the one 'at Jim was sweet
    on,
An' Cyrus Jones an' Mandy Smith an' Faith an' Patience
    Deaton.
Then Parson Brown an' Lawyer Jones were present—all
    attention,
An' piles on piles of other folks too numerous to mention.
The master rose an' briefly said: "Good friends, dear brother
    Crawford,
To spur the pupils' minds along, a little prize has offered.
To him who spells the best tonight—or 't may be 'her'—no
    tellin'—
He offers ez a jest reward, this precious work on spellin'."
A little blue-backed spellin'-book with fancy scarlet trimmin';
We boys devoured it with our eyes—so did the girls an'
    women.
He held it up where all could see, then on the table set it,
An' ev'ry speller in the house felt mortal bound to get it.
At his command we fell in line, prepared to do our dooty,
Outspell the rest an' set 'em down, an' carry home the booty.
'Twas then the merry times began, the blunders, an' the laffin',
The nudges an' the nods an' winks an' stale good-natured
    chaffin'.
Ole Uncle Hiram Dane was there, the clostest man a-livin',
Whose only bugbear seemed to be the dreadful fear o' givin'.
His beard was long, his hair uncut, his clothes all bare an'
    dingy;
It wasn't 'cause the man was pore, but jest so mortal stingy;
An' there he sot by Sally Riggs a-smilin' an' a-smirkin',
An' all his children lef' to home a diggin' an' a-workin'.
A widower he was, an' Sal was thinkin' 'at she'd wing him;
I reckon he was wond'rin' what them rings o' hern would
    bring him.
An' when the spellin'-test commenced, he up an' took his
    station,
A-spellin' with the best o' them to beat the very nation.

An' when he'd spell some youngster down, he'd turn to look
    at Sally,
An' say: "The teachin' nowadays can't be o' no great vally."
But true enough the adage says, "Pride walks in slipp'ry
    places,"
Fur soon a thing occurred that put a smile on all our faces.
The laffter jest kep' ripplin' 'roun' an' teacher couldn't quell it,
Fur when he give out "charity" ole Hiram couldn't spell it.
But laffin' 's ketchin' an' it throwed some others off their
    bases,
An' folks 'u'd miss the very word that seemed to fit their
    cases.
Why, fickle little Jessie Lee come near the house upsettin'
By puttin' in a double "kay" to spell the word "coquettin'."
An' when it come to Cyrus Jones, it tickled me all over—
Him settin' up to Mandy Smith an' got sot down on "lover."
But Lawyer Jones of all gone men did shorely look the gonest,
When he found out that he'd furgot to put the "h" in
    "honest."
An' Parson Brown, whose sermons were too long fur
    toleration,
Caused lots o' smiles by missin' when they give out
    "condensation."
So one by one they giv' it up—the big words kep' a-landin',
Till me an' Nettie Gray was left, the only ones a-standin',
An' then my inward strife began—I guess my mind was
    petty—
I did so want that spellin'-book; but then to spell down Nettie
Jest sort o' went ag'in my grain—I somehow couldn't do it,
An' when I git a notion fixed, I'm great on stickin' to it.
So when they giv' the next word out—I hadn't orter tell it,
But then 'twas all fur Nettie's sake—I missed so's she could
    spell it.
She spelt the word, then looked at me so lovin'-like an' mello',
I tell you 't sent a hundred pins a shootin' through a fello'.
O' course I had to stand the jokes an' chaffin' of the fello's,
But when they handed her the book I vow I wasn't jealous.
We sung a hymn, an' Parson Brown dismissed us like he orter,

From the greatest to the least,
None are from the rule released.
Be thou toiler, poet, priest,
    Keep a-pluggin' away.

Delve away beneath the surface,
There is treasure farther down,—
    Keep a-pluggin' away.
Let the rain come down in torrents,
Let the threat'ning heavens frown,
    Keep a-pluggin' away.
When the clouds have rolled away,
There will come a brighter day
All your labor to repay,—
    Keep a-pluggin' away.

There'll be lots of sneers to swallow,
There'll be lots of pain to bear,—
    Keep a-pluggin' away.
If you've got your eye on heaven,
Some bright day you'll wake up there,—
    Keep a-pluggin' away.
Perseverance still is king;
Time its sure reward will bring;
Work and wait unwearying,—
    Keep a-pluggin' away.

An Easy-Goin' Feller

Ther' ain't no use in all this strife,
An' hurryin', pell-mell, right thro' life.
I don't believe in goin' too fast
To see what kind o' road you've passed.
It ain't no mortal kind o' good,
'N' I wouldn't hurry ef I could.
I like to jest go joggin' 'long,
To limber up my soul with song;

To stop awhile 'n' chat the men,
'N' drink some cider now an' then.
Do' want no boss a-standin' by
To see me work; I allus try
To do my dooty right straight up,
An' earn what fills my plate an' cup.
An' ez fur boss, I'll be my own,
I like to jest be let alone,
To plough my strip an' tend my bees,
An' do jest like I doggoned please.
My head's all right, an' my heart's meller,
But I'm a easy-goin' feller.

The Wooing

A youth went faring up and down,
    Alack and well-a-day.
He fared him to the market town,
    Alack and well-a-day.
And there he met a maiden fair,
With hazel eyes and auburn hair;
His heart went from him then and there,
    Alack and well-a-day.

She posies sold right merrily,
    Alack and well-a-day;
But not a flower was fair as she,
    Alack and well-a-day.
He bought a rose and sighed a sigh,
"Ah, dearest maiden, would that I
Might dare the seller too to buy!"
    Alack and well-a-day.

She tossed her head, the coy coquette,
    Alack and well-a-day.
"I'm not, sir, in the market yet,"
    Alack and well-a-day.

"Your love must cool upon a shelf;
Tho' much I sell for gold and pelf,
I'm yet too young to sell myself,"
    Alack and well-a-day.

The youth was filled with sorrow sore,
    Alack and well-a-day.
And looked he at the maid once more,
    Alack and well-a-day.
Then loud he cried, "Fair maiden, if
Too young to sell, now as I live,
You're not too young yourself to give,"
    Alack and well-a-day.

The little maid cast down her eyes,
    Alack and well-a-day.
And many a flush began to rise,
    Alack and well-a-day.
"Why, since you are so bold," she said,
"I doubt not you are highly bred,
So take me!" and the twain were wed,
    Alack and well-a-day.

When de Co'n Pone's Hot

Dey is times in life when Nature
    Seems to slip a cog an' go,
Jes' a-rattlin' down creation,
    Lak an ocean's overflow;
When de worl' jes' stahts a-spinnin'
Lak a picaninny's top,
An' yo' cup o' joy is brimmin'
    'Twell it seems about to slop,
An' you feel jes' lak a racah,

Dat is trainin' fu' to trot—
When yo' mammy says de blessin'
　An' de co'n pone's hot.

When you set down at de table,
　Kin' o' weary lak an' sad,
An' you'se jes' a little tiahed
　An' purhaps a little mad;
How yo' gloom tu'ns into gladness,
　How yo' joy drives out de doubt
When de oven do' is opened,
　An' de smell comes po'in' out;
Why, de 'lectric light o' Heaven
　Seems to settle on de spot,
When yo' mammy says de blessin'
　An' de co'n pone's hot.

When de cabbage pot is steamin'
　An' de bacon good an' fat,
When de chittlins is a-sputter'n'
　So's to show you whah dey's at;
Tek away yo' sody biscuit,
　Tek away yo' cake an' pie,
Fu' de glory time is comin',
　An' it's 'proachin' mighty nigh,
An' you want to jump an' hollah,
　Dough you know you'd bettah not,
When yo' mammy says de blessin'
　An' de co'n pone's hot.

I have hyeahd o' lots o' sermons,
　An' I've hyeahd o' lots o' prayers,
An' I've listened to some singin'
　Dat has tuck me up de stairs
Of de Glory-Lan' an' set me
　Jes' below de Mastah's th'one,
An' have lef' my hea't a-singin'
　In a happy aftah tone;

But dem wu'ds so sweetly murmured
   Seem to tech de softes' spot,
When my mammy says de blessin',
   An' de co'n pone's hot.

Discovered

Seen you down at chu'ch las' night,
   Nevah min', Miss Lucy.
What I mean? oh, dat's all right,
   Nevah min', Miss Lucy.
You was sma't ez sma't could be,
But you couldn't hide f'om me.
Ain't I got two eyes to see!
   Nevah min', Miss Lucy.

Guess you thought you's awful keen;
   Nevah min', Miss Lucy.
Evahthing you done, I seen;
   Nevah min', Miss Lucy.
Seen him tek yo' ahm jes' so,
When he got outside de do'—
Oh, I know dat man's yo' beau!
   Nevah min', Miss Lucy.

Say now, honey, wha'd he say?—
   Nevah min', Miss Lucy!
Keep yo' secrets—dat's yo' way—
   Nevah min', Miss Lucy.
Won't tell me an' I'm yo' pal—
I'm gwine tell his othah gal,—
Know huh, too, huh name is Sal;
   Nevah min', Miss Lucy!

The Delinquent

Goo'-by, Jinks, I got to hump,
Got to mek dis pony jump;
See dat sun a-goin' down
'N' me a-foolin' hyeah in town!
    Git up, Suke—go long!

Guess Mirandy'll think I's tight,
Me not home an' comin' on night.
What's dat stan'in' by de fence?
Pshaw! why don't I lu'n some sense?
    Git up, Suke—go long!

Guess I spent down dah at Jinks'
Mos' a dollah fur de drinks.
Bless yo'r soul, you see dat star?
Lawd, but won't Mirandy rar?
    Git up, Suke—go long!

Went dis mo'nin', hyeah it's night,
Dah's de cabin dah in sight.
Who's dat stan'in' in de do'?
Dat must be Mirandy, sho',
    Git up, Suke—go long!

Got de close-stick in huh han',
Dat look funny, goodness lan',
Sakes alibe, but she look glum!
Hyeah, Mirandy, hyeah I come!
    Git up, Suke—go long!

Ef 't hadn't a' b'en fur you, you
slow ole fool, I'd a' be'n home
long fo' now!

A Confidence

Uncle John, he makes me tired;
Thinks 'at he's jest so all-fired
Smart, 'at he kin pick up, so,
Ever'thing he wants to know.
Tried to ketch me up last night,
But you bet I wouldn't bite.
I jest kep' the smoothes' face,
But I led him sich a chase,
Couldn't corner me, you bet—
I skipped all the traps he set.
Makin' out he wan'ed to know
Who was this an' that girl's beau;
So's he'd find out, don't you see,
Who was goin' 'long with me.
But I answers jest ez sly,
An' I never winks my eye,
Tell he hollers with a whirl,
"Look here, ain't you got a girl?"
Y' ought 'o seen me spread my eyes,
Like he'd took me by surprise,
An' I said, "Oh, Uncle John,
Never thought o' havin' one."
An' somehow that seemed to tickle
Him an' he shelled out a nickel.
Then you ought to seen me leave
Jest a-laffin' in my sleeve.
Fool him—well, I guess I did;
He ain't on to this here kid.
Got a girl! well, I guess yes,
Got a dozen more or less,
But I got one reely one,
Not no foolin' ner no fun;
Fur I'm sweet on her, you see,

An' I ruther guess 'at she
Must be kinder sweet on me,
So we're keepin' company.
Honest Injun! this is true,
Ever' word I'm tellin' you!
But you won't be sich a scab
Ez to run aroun' an' blab.
Mebbe 'tain't the way with you,
But you know some fellers do.
Spoils a girl to let her know
'At you talk about her so.
Don't you know her? her name's Liz,
Nicest girl in town she is.
Purty? ah, git out, you gilly—
Liz 'ud purt 'nigh knock you silly.
Y' ought 'o see her when she's dressed
All up in her Sunday best,
All the fellers nudgin' me,
An' a-whisperin', gemunee!
Betcher life 'at I feel proud
When she passes by the crowd.
'T's kinder nice to be a-goin'
With a girl 'at makes some showin'—
One you know 'at hain't no snide,
Makes you feel so satisfied.
An' I'll tell you she's a trump,
Never even seen her jump
Like some silly girls 'ud do,
When I'd hide and holler "Boo!"
She'd jest laff an' say "Git out!
What you hollerin' about?"
When some girls 'ud have a fit
That 'un don't git skeered a bit,
Never makes a bit o' row
When she sees a worm er cow.
Them kind's few an' far between;
Bravest girl I ever seen.
Tell you 'nuther thing she'll do,

Mebbe you won't think it's true,
But if she's jest got a dime
She'll go halvers ever' time.
Ah, you goose, you needn't laff;
That's the kinder girl to have.
If you knowed her like I do,
Guess you'd kinder like her too.
Tell you somep'n' if you'll swear
You won't tell it anywhere.
Oh, you got to cross yer heart
Earnest, truly, 'fore I start.
Well, one day I kissed her cheek
Gee, but I felt cheap an' weak,
'Cause at first she kinder flared,
'N', gracious goodness! I was scared.
But I needn't been, fer la!
Why, she never told her ma.
That's what I call grit, don't you?
Sich a girl's worth stickin' to.

The Party

Dey had a gread big pahty down to Tom's de othah night;
Was I dah? You bet! I nevah in my life see sich a sight;
All de folks f'om fou' plantations was invited, an' dey come,
Dey come troopin' thick ez chillun when dey hyeahs a fife an'
     drum.
Evahbody dressed deir fines'—Heish yo' mouf an' git away,
Ain't seen no sich fancy dressin' sence las' quah'tly meetin'
     day;
Gals all dressed in silks an' satins, not a wrinkle ner a crease,
Eyes a-battin', teeth a-shinin', haih breshed back ez slick ez
     grease;
Sku'ts all tucked an' puffed an' ruffled, evah blessed seam an'
     stitch;
Ef you'd seen 'em wif deir mistus, couldn't swahed to which
     was which.

Men all dressed up in Prince Alberts, swaller-tails 'u'd tek yo'
    bref!
I cain't tell you nothin' 'bout it, y' ought to seen it fu' yo'se'f.
Who was dah? Now who you askin'? How you 'spect I gwine
    to know?
You mus' think I stood an' counted evahbody at de do'.
Ole man Babah's house-boy Isaac, brung dat gal, Malindy Jane,
Huh a-hangin' to his elbow, him a-struttin' wif a cane;
My, but Hahvey Jones was jealous! seemed to stick him lak a
    tho'n;
But he laughed with Viney Cahteh, tryin' ha'd to not let on,
But a pusson would'a' noticed f'om de d'rection of his look,
Dat he was watchin' ev'ry step dat Ike an' Lindy took.
Ike he foun' a cheer an' asked huh: "Won't you set down?"
    wif a smile,
An' she answe'd up a-bowin', "Oh, I reckon 'tain't wuth
    while."
Dat was jes' fu' style, I reckon, 'cause she sot down jes' de
    same,
An' she stayed dah 'twell he fetched huh fu' to jine some so't
    o' game;
Den I hyeahd huh sayin' propah, ez she riz to go away,
"Oh, you raly mus' excuse me, fu' I hardly keers to play."
But I seen huh in a minute wif de othahs on de flo',
An' dah wasn't any one o' dem a-playin' any mo';
Comin' down de flo' a-bowin' an' a-swayin' an' a-swingin',
Puttin' on huh high-toned mannahs all de time dat she was
    singin':
"Oh, swing Johnny up an' down, swing him all aroun',
Swing Johnny up an' down, swing him all aroun',
Oh, swing Johnny up an' down, swing him all aroun'
Fa' you well, my dahlin'."
Had to laff at ole man Johnson, he's a caution now, you bet—
Hittin' clost onto a hunderd, but he's spry an' nimble yet;
He 'lowed how a-so't o' gigglin', "I ain't ole, I'll let you see,
D'ain't no use in gittin' feeble, now you youngstahs jes' watch
    me,"

An' he grabbed ole Aunt Marier—weighs th'ee hunderd mo'
    er less,
An' he spun huh 'roun' de cabin swingin' Johnny lak de res'.
Evahbody laffed an' hollahed: "Go it! Swing huh, Uncle Jim!"
An' he swung huh too, I reckon, lak a youngstah, who but
    him.
Dat was bettah'n young Scott Thomas, tryin' to be so awful
    smaht.
You know when dey gits to singin' an' dey comes to dat ere
    paht:

    "In some lady's new brick house,
    In some lady's gyahden.
    Ef you don't let me out, I will jump out,
    So fa' you well, my dahlin'."

Den dey's got a circle 'roun' you, an' you's got to break de
    line;
Well, dat dahky was so anxious, lak to bust hisse'f a-tryin';
Kep' on blund'rin' 'roun' an' foolin' 'twell he giv' one gread
    big jump,
Broke de line, an lit head-fo'most in de fiah-place right plump;
Hit 'ad fiah in it, mind you; well, I thought my soul I'd bust,
Tried my best to keep f'om laffin', but hit seemed like die I
    must!
Y' ought to seen dat man a-scramblin' f'om de ashes an' de
    grime.
Did it bu'n him! Sich a question, why he didn't give it time;
Th'ow'd dem ashes and dem cindahs evah which-a-way I
    guess,
An' you nevah did, I reckon, clap yo' eyes on sich a mess;
Fu' he sholy made a picter an' a funny one to boot,
Wif his clothes all full o' ashes an' his face all full o' soot.
Well, hit laked to stopped de pahty, an' I reckon lak ez not
Dat it would ef Tom's wife, Mandy, hadn't happened on de
    spot,
To invite us out to suppah—well, we scrambled to de table,
An' I'd lak to tell you 'bout it—what we had—but I ain't able,

Mention jes' a few things, dough I know I hadn't orter,
Fu' I know 'twill staht a hank'rin' an' yo' mouf'll 'mence to
    worter.
We had wheat bread white ez cotton an' a egg pone jes like
    gol',
Hog jole, bilin' hot an' steamin' roasted shoat an' ham sliced
    cold—
Look out! What's de mattah wif you? Don't be fallin' on de
    flo';
Ef it's go'n' to 'fect you dat way, I won't tell you nothin' mo'.
Dah now—well, we had hot chittlin's—now you's tryin' ag'in
    to fall,
Cain't you stan' to hyeah about it? S'pose you'd been an' seed
    it all;
Seed dem gread big sweet pertaters, layin' by de possum's side,
Seed dat coon in all his gravy, reckon den you'd up and died!
Mandy 'lowed "you all mus' 'scuse me, d' wa'n't much upon
    my she'ves,
But I's done my bes' to suit you, so set down an' he'p
    yo'se'ves."
Tom, he 'lowed: "I don't b'lieve in 'pologisin' an' perfessin',
Let 'em tek it lak dey ketch it. Eldah Thompson, ask de
    blessin'."
Wish you'd seed dat colo'ed preachah cleah his th'oat an' bow
    his head;
One eye shet, an' one eye open,—dis is evah wud he said:
"Lawd, look down in tendah mussy on sich generous hea'ts ez
    dese;
Make us truly thankful, amen. Pass dat possum, ef you
    please!"
Well, we eat and drunk ouah po'tion, 'twell dah wasn't
    nothin' lef,
An' we felt jes' like new sausage, we was mos' nigh stuffed to
    def!
Tom, he knowed how we'd be feelin', so he had de fiddlah
    'roun',
An' he made us cleah de cabin fu' to dance dat suppah down.
Jim, de fiddlah, chuned his fiddle, put some rosum on his bow,

Set a pine box on de table, mounted it an' let huh go!
He's a fiddlah, now I tell you, an' he made dat fiddle ring,
'Twell de ol'est an' de lamest had to give deir feet a fling.
Jigs, cotillions, reels an' breakdowns, cordrills an' a waltz er
    two;
Bless yo' soul, dat music winged 'em an' dem people lak to
    flew.
Cripple Joe, de old rheumatic, danced dat flo' f'om side to
    middle,
Th'owed away his crutch an' hopped it; what's rheumatics
    'ginst a fiddle?
Eldah Thompson got so tickled dat he lak to los' his grace,
Had to tek bofe feet an' hol' dem so's to keep 'em in deir
    place.
An' de Christuns an' de sinnahs got so mixed up on dat flo',
Dat I don't see how dey'd pahted ef de trump had chanced to
    blow.
Well, we danced dat way an' capahed in de mos' redic'lous
    way,
'Twell de roostahs in de bahnyard cleahed deir th'oats an'
    crowed fu' day.
Y' ought to been dah, fu' I tell you evahthing was rich an'
    prime,
An' dey ain't no use in talkin', we jes had one scrumptious
    time!

FROM *POEMS OF CABIN AND FIELD*
1899

The Deserted Plantation

Oh, de grubbin'-hoe's a-rustin' in de co'nah,
    An' de plow's a-tumblin' down in de fiel',
While de whippo'will's a-wailin' lak a mou'nah
    When his stubbo'n hea't is tryin' ha'd to yiel'.

In de furrers whah de co'n was allus wavin',
    Now de weeds is growin' green an' rank an' tall;
An' de swallers roun' de whole place is a-bravin'
    Lak dey thought deir folks had allus owned it all.

An' de big house stan's all quiet lak an' solemn,
    Not a blessed soul in pa'lor, po'ch, er lawn;
Not a guest, ner not a ca'iage lef' to haul 'em,
    Fu' de ones dat tu'ned de latch-string out air gone.

An' de banjo's voice is silent in de qua'ters,
    D' ain't a hymn ner co'n-song ringin' in de air;
But de murmur of a branch's passin' waters
    Is de only soun' dat breks de stillness dere.

Whah's de da'kies, dem dat used to be a-dancin'
    Ev'ry night befo' de ole cabin do'?
Whah's de chillun, dem dat used to be a-prancin'
    Er a-rollin' in de san' er on de flo'?

Whah's ole Uncle Mordecai an' Uncle Aaron?
    Whah's Aunt Doshy, Sam, an' Kit, an' all de res'?
Whah's ole Tom de da'ky fiddlah, how's he farin'?
    Whah's de gals dat used to sing an' dance de bes'?

Gone! not one o' dem is lef' to tell de story;
   Dey have lef' de deah ole place to fall away.
Couldn't one o' dem dat seed it in its glory
   Stay to watch it in de hour of decay?

Dey have lef' de ole plantation to de swallers,
   But it hol's in me a lover till de las';
Fu' I fin' hyeah in de memory dat follers
   All dat loved me an' dat I loved in de pas'.

So I'll stay an' watch de deah ole place an' tend it
   Ez I used to in de happy days gone by.
'Twell de othah Mastah thinks it's time to end it,
   An' calls me to my qua'ters in de sky.

Little Brown Baby

Little brown baby wif spa'klin' eyes,
   Come to yo' pappy an' set on his knee.
What you been doin', suh—makin' san' pies?
   Look at dat bib—you's ez du'ty ez me.
Look at dat mouf—dat's merlasses, I bet;
   Come hyeah, Maria, an' wipe off his han's.
Bees gwine to ketch you an' eat you up yit,
   Bein' so sticky an sweet—goodness lan's!

Little brown baby wif spa'klin' eyes,
   Who's pappy's darlin' an' who's pappy's chile?
Who is it all de day nevah once tries
   Fu' to be cross, er once loses dat smile?
Whah did you git dem teef? My, you's a scamp!
   Whah did dat dimple come f'om in yo' chin?
Pappy do' know you—I b'lieves you's a tramp;
   Mammy, dis hyeah's some ol' straggler got in!

Let's th'ow him outen de do' in de san',
   We do' want stragglers a-layin' 'roun' hyeah;
Let's gin him 'way to de big buggah-man;
   I know he's hidin' erroun' hyeah right neah.
Buggah-man, buggah-man, come in de do',
   Hyeah's a bad boy you kin have fu' to eat.
Mammy an' pappy do' want him no mo',
   Swaller him down f'om his haid to his feet!

Dah, now, I t'ought dat you'd hug me up close.
   Go back, ol' buggah, you sha'n't have dis boy.
He ain't no tramp, ner no straggler, of co'se;
   He's pappy's pa'dner an' playmate an' joy.
Come to you' pallet now—go to yo' res';
   Wisht you could allus know ease an' cleah skies;
Wisht you could stay jes' a chile on my breas'—
   Little brown baby wif spa'klin' eyes!

Chrismus Is A-Comin'

Bones a-gittin' achy,
Back a-feelin' col',
Han's a-growin' shaky,
Jes' lak I was ol'.
Fros' erpon de meddah
Lookin' mighty white;
Snowdraps lak a feddah
Slippin' down at night.
Jes' keep t'ings a-hummin'
Spite o' fros' an' showahs,
Chrismus is a-comin'
An' all de week is ouahs.

Little mas' a-axin',
"Who is Santy Claus?"
Meks it kin' o' taxin'
Not to brek de laws.

Chillun's pow'ful tryin'
To a pusson's grace
W'en dey go a pryin'
Right on th'oo you' face
Down ermong yo' feelin's;
Jes' 'pears lak dat you
Got to change you' dealin's
So's to tell 'em true.

An' my pickaninny—
Dreamin' in his sleep!
Come hyeah, Mammy Jinny,
Come an' tek a peep.
Ol' Mas' Bob an' Missis
In dey house up daih
Got no chile lak dis is,
D' ain't none anywhaih.
Sleep, my little lammy,
Sleep, you little limb,
He do' know whut mammy
Done saved up fu' him.

Dey'll be banjo pickin',
Dancin' all night thoo.
Dey'll be lots o' chicken,
Plenty tukky, too.
Drams to wet yo' whistles
So's to drive out chills.
Whut I keer fu' drizzles
Fallin' on de hills?
Jes' keep t'ings a-hummin'
Spite o' col' an' showahs,
Chrismus day's a-comin',
An' all de week is ouahs.

FROM *LYRICS OF THE HEARTHSIDE*
1899

Love's Apotheosis

Love me. I care not what the circling years
    To me may do.
If, but in spite of time and tears,
    You prove but true.

Love me—albeit grief shall dim mine eyes,
    And tears bedew,
I shall not e'en complain, for then my skies
    Shall still be blue.

Love me, and though the winter snow shall pile,
    And leave me chill,
Thy passion's warmth shall make for me, meanwhile,
    A sun-kissed hill.

And when the days have lengthened into years,
    And I grow old,
Oh, spite of pains and griefs and cares and fears,
    Grow thou not cold.

Then hand and hand we shall pass up the hill,
    I say not down;
That twain go up, of love, who've loved their fill,—
    To gain love's crown.

Love me, and let my life take up thine own,
    As sun the dew.
Come, sit, my queen, for in my heart a throne
    Awaits for you!

The Paradox

I am the mother of sorrows,
    I am the ender of grief;
I am the bud and the blossom,
    I am the late-falling leaf.

I am thy priest and thy poet,
    I am thy serf and thy king;
I cure the tears of the heartsick,
    When I come near they shall sing.

White are my hands as the snowdrop;
    Swart are my fingers as clay;
Dark is my frown as the midnight,
    Fair is my brow as the day.

Battle and war are my minions,
    Doing my will as divine;
I am the calmer of passions,
    Peace is a nursling of mine.

Speak to me gently or curse me,
    Seek me or fly from my sight;
I am thy fool in the morning,
    Thou art my slave in the night.

Down to the grave will I take thee,
    Out from the noise of the strife;
Then shalt thou see me and know me—
    Death, then, no longer, but life.

Then shalt thou sing at my coming,
  Kiss me with passionate breath,
Clasp me and smile to have thought me
  Aught save the foeman of Death.

Come to me, brother, when weary,
  Come when thy lonely heart swells;
I'll guide thy footsteps and lead thee
  Down where the Dream Woman dwells.

The Right to Die

I have no fancy for that ancient cant
That makes us masters of our destinies,
And not our lives, to hold or give them up
As will directs; I cannot, will not think
That men, the subtle worms, who plot and plan
And scheme and calculate with such shrewd wit,
Are such great blund'ring fools as not to know
When they have lived enough.
                    Men court not death
When there are sweets still left in life to taste.
Nor will a brave man choose to live when he,
Full deeply drunk of life, has reached the dregs,
And knows that now but bitterness remains.
He is the coward who, outfaced in this,
Fears the false goblins of another life.
I honor him who being much harassed
Drinks of sweet courage until drunk of it,—
Then seizing Death, reluctant, by the hand,
Leaps with him, fearless, to eternal peace!

Behind the Arras

As in some dim baronial hall restrained,
A prisoner sits, engirt by secret doors
And waving tapestries that argue forth
Strange passages into the outer air;
So in this dimmer room which we call life,
Thus sits the soul and marks with eye intent
That mystic curtain o'er the portal death;
Still deeming that behind the arras lies
The lambent way that leads to lasting light.
Poor fooled and foolish soul! Know now that death
Is but a blind, false door that nowhere leads,
And gives no hope of exit final, free.

A Hymn
After Reading Lead, Kindly Light.

Lead gently, Lord, and slow,
   For oh, my steps are weak,
And ever as I go,
   Some soothing sentence speak;

That I may turn my face
   Through doubt's obscurity
Toward thine abiding-place,
   E'en tho' I cannot see.

For lo, the way is dark;
   Through mist and cloud I grope,
Save for that fitful spark,
   The little flame of hope.

Lead gently, Lord, and slow,
　　For fear that I may fall;
I know not where to go
　　Unless I hear thy call.

My fainting soul doth yearn
　　For thy green hills afar;
So let thy mercy burn—
　　My greater, guiding star!

Dream Song I

Long years ago, within a distant clime,
Ere Love had touched me with his wand sublime,
I dreamed of one to make my life's calm May
The panting passion of a summer's day.
And ever since, in almost sad suspense,
I have been waiting with a soul intense
To greet and take unto myself the beams,
Of her, my star, the lady of my dreams.

O Love, still longed and looked for, come to me,
Be thy far home by mountain, vale, or sea.
My yearning heart may never find its rest
Until thou liest rapt upon my breast.
The wind may bring its perfume from the south,
Is it so sweet as breath from my love's mouth?
Oh, naught that surely is, and naught that seems
May turn me from the lady of my dreams.

Dream Song II

Pray, what can dreams avail
　　To make love or to mar?
The child within the cradle rail

Lies dreaming of the star.
But is the star by this beguiled
To leave its place and seek the child?

The poor plucked rose within its glass
    Still dreameth of the bee;
But, tho' the lagging moments pass,
    Her Love she may not see.
If dream of child and flower fail,
Why should a maiden's dreams prevail?

The King Is Dead

Aye, lay him in his grave, the old dead year!
His life is lived—fulfilled his destiny.
Have you for him no sad, regretful tear
To drop beside the cold, unfollowed bier?
Can you not pay the tribute of a sigh?

Was he not kind to you, this dead old year?
Did he not give enough of earthly store?
Enough of love, and laughter, and good cheer?
Have not the skies you scanned sometimes been clear?
How, then, of him who dies, could you ask more?

It is not well to hate him for the pain
He brought you, and the sorrows manifold.
To pardon him these hurts still I am fain;
For in the panting period of his reign,
He brought me new wounds, but he healed the old.

One little sigh for thee, my poor, dead friend—
One little sigh while my companions sing.
Thou art so soon forgotten in the end;
We cry e'en as thy footsteps downward tend:
"The king is dead! long live the king!"

Theology

There is a heaven, for ever, day by day,
The upward longing of my soul doth tell me so.
There is a hell, I'm quite as sure; for pray,
If there were not, where would my neighbours go?

Resignation

Long had I grieved at what I deemed abuse;
   But now I am as grain within the mill.
If so be thou must crush me for thy use,
   Grind on, O potent God, and do thy will!

Thou Art My Lute

Thou art my lute, by thee I sing,—
   My being is attuned to thee.
Thou settest all my words a-wing,
   And meltest me to melody.

Thou art my life, by thee I live,
   From thee proceed the joys I know;
Sweetheart, thy hand has power to give
   The meed of love—the cup of woe.

Thou art my love, by thee I lead
   My soul the paths of light along,
From vale to vale, from mead to mead,
   And home it in the hills of song.

My song, my soul, my life, my all,
    Why need I pray or make my plea,
Since my petition cannot fall;
    For I'm already one with thee!

The Phantom Kiss

One night in my room, still and beamless,
    With will and with thought in eclipse,
I rested in sleep that was dreamless;
    When softly there fell on my lips

A touch, as of lips that were pressing
    Mine own with the message of bliss—
A sudden, soft, fleeting caressing,
    A breath like a maiden's first kiss.

I woke—and the scoffer may doubt me—
    I peered in surprise through the gloom;
But nothing and none were about me,
    And I was alone in my room.

Perhaps 'twas the wind that caressed me
    And touched me with dew-laden breath;
Or, maybe, close-sweeping, there passed me
    The low-winging Angel of Death.

Some sceptic may choose to disdain it,
    Or one feign to read it aright;
Or wisdom may seek to explain it—
    This mystical kiss in the night.

But rather let fancy thus clear it;
    That, thinking of me here alone,
The miles were made naught, and, in spirit,
    Thy lips, love, were laid on mine own.

The Crisis

A man of low degree was sore oppressed,
  Fate held him under iron-handed sway,
And ever, those who saw him thus distressed
  Would bid him bend his stubborn will and pray.
But he, strong in himself and obdurate,
Waged, prayerless, on his losing fight with Fate.

Friends gave his proffered hand their coldest clasp,
  Or took it not at all; and Poverty,
That bruised his body with relentless grasp,
  Grinned, taunting, when he struggled to be free.
But though with helpless hands he beat the air,
His need extreme yet found no voice in prayer.

Then he prevailed; and forthwith snobbish Fate,
  Like some whipped cur, came fawning at his feet;
Those who had scorned forgave and called him great—
  His friends found out that friendship still was sweet.
But he, once obdurate, now bowed his head
In prayer, and trembling with its import, said:

"Mere human strength may stand ill-fortune's frown;
  So I prevailed, for human strength was mine;
But from the killing pow'r of great renown,
  Naught may protect me save a strength divine.
Help me, O Lord, in this my trembling cause;
I scorn men's curses, but I dread applause!"

Alexander Crummell Dead

Back to the breast of thy mother,
Child of the earth!
E'en her caress can not smother
What thou hast done.
Follow the trail of the westering sun
Over the earth.
Thy light and his were as one—
Sun, in thy worth.
Unto a nation whose sky was as night,
Camest thou, holily, bearing thy light:
And the dawn came,
In it thy fame
Flashed up in a flame.

Back to the breast of thy mother—
To rest.
Long hast thou striven;
Dared where the hills by the lightning of heaven were riven;
Go now, pure shriven.
Who shall come after thee, out of the clay—
Learned one and leader to show us the way?
Who shall rise up when the world gives the test?
Think thou no more of this—
Rest!

Sonnet
On an Old Book with Uncut Leaves

Emblem of blasted hope and lost desire,
   No finger ever traced thy yellow page
   Save Time's. Thou hast not wrought to noble rage
The hearts thou wouldst have stirred. Not any fire

Save sad flames set to light a funeral pyre
   Dost thou suggest. Nay,—impotent in age,
   Unsought, thou holdst a corner of the stage
And ceasest even dumbly to aspire.

How different was the thought of him that writ.
   What promised he to love of ease and wealth,
When men should read and kindle at his wit.
   But here decay eats up the book by stealth,
While it, like some old maiden, solemnly,
Hugs its incongruous virginity!

Misapprehension

Out of my heart, one day, I wrote a song,
   With my heart's blood imbued,
Instinct with passion, tremulously strong,
   With grief subdued;
   Breathing a fortitude
     Pain-bought.
And one who claimed much love for what I wrought,
   Read and considered it,
     And spoke:
"Ay, brother,—'tis well writ,
     But where's the joke?"

For the Man Who Fails

The world is a snob, and the man who wins
   Is the chap for its money's worth:
And the lust for success causes half of the sins
   That are cursing this brave old earth.
For it's fine to go up, and the world's applause
   Is sweet to the mortal ear;
But the man who fails in a noble cause
   Is a hero that's no less dear.

'Tis true enough that the laurel crown
   Twines but for the victor's brow;
For many a hero has lain him down
   With naught but the cypress bough.
There are gallant men in the losing fight,
   And as gallant deeds are done
As ever graced the captured height
   Or the battle grandly won.

We sit at life's board with our nerves highstrung,
   And we play for the stake of Fame,
And our odes are sung and our banners hung
   For the man who wins the game.
But I have a song of another kind
   Than breathes in these fame-wrought gales,—
An ode to the noble heart and mind
   Of the gallant man who fails!

The man who is strong to fight his fight,
   And whose will no front can daunt,
If the truth be truth and the right be right,
   Is the man that the ages want.
Tho' he fail and die in grim defeat,
   Yet he has not fled the strife,
And the house of Earth will seem more sweet
   For the perfume of his life.

Harriet Beecher Stowe

She told the story, and the whole world wept
   At wrongs and cruelties it had not known
   But for this fearless woman's voice alone.
   She spoke to consciences that long had slept:
Her message, Freedom's clear reveille, swept
   From heedless hovel to complacent throne.
   Command and prophecy were in the tone
   And from its sheath the sword of justice leapt.

Around two peoples swelled a fiery wave,
  But both came forth transfigured from the flame.
Blest be the hand that dared be strong to save,
  And blest be she who in our weakness came—
  Prophet and priestess! At one stroke she gave
  A race to freedom and herself to fame.

The Warrior's Prayer

Long since, in sore distress, I heard one pray,
  "Lord, who prevailest with resistless might,
Ever from war and strife keep me away,
  My battles fight!"

I know not if I play the Pharisee,
  And if my brother after all be right;
But mine shall be the warrior's plea to thee—
  Strength for the fight.

I do not ask that thou shalt front the fray,
  And drive the warring foeman from my sight;
I only ask, O Lord, by night, by day,
  Strength for the fight!

When foes upon me press, let me not quail
  Nor think to turn me into coward flight.
I only ask, to make mine arms prevail,
  Strength for the fight!

Still let mine eyes look ever on the foe,
  Still let mine armor case me strong and bright;
And grant me, as I deal each righteous blow,
  Strength for the fight!

And when, at eventide, the fray is done,
    My soul to Death's bedchamber do thou light,
And give me, be the field or lost or won,
    Rest from the fight!

The Voice of the Banjo

In a small and lonely cabin out of noisy traffic's way,
Sat an old man, bent and feeble, dusk of face, and hair of
    gray,
And beside him on the table, battered, old, and worn as he,
Lay a banjo, droning forth this reminiscent melody:

"Night is closing in upon us, friend of mine, but don't be sad;
Let us think of all the pleasures and the joys that we have had.
Let us keep a merry visage, and be happy till the last,
Let the future still be sweetened with the honey of the past.

"For I speak to you of summer nights upon the yellow sand,
When the Southern moon was sailing high and silvering all the
    land;
And if love tales were not sacred, there's a tale that I could tell
Of your many nightly wanderings with a dusk and lovely
    belle.

"And I speak to you of care-free songs when labour's hour
    was o'er,
And a woman waiting for your step outside the cabin door,
And of something roly-poly that you took upon your lap,
While you listened for the stumbling, hesitating words,
    'Pap, pap.'

"I could tell you of a 'possum hunt across the wooded
    grounds,
I could call to mind the sweetness of the baying of the hounds,
You could lift me up and smelling of the timber that's in me,
Build again a whole green forest with the mem'ry of a tree.

"So the future cannot hurt us while we keep the past in mind,
What care I for trembling fingers,—what care you that you
    are blind?
Time may leave us poor and stranded, circumstance may
    make us bend;
But they'll only find us mellower, won't they, comrade?—in
    the end."

A Choice

They please me not—these solemn songs
That hint of sermons covered up.
'Tis true the world should heed its wrongs,
    But in a poem let me sup,
Not simples brewed to cure or ease
Humanity's confessed disease,
But the spirit-wine of a singing line,
    Or a dew-drop in a honey cup!

The Real Question

Folks is talkin' 'bout de money, 'bout de silvah an' de gold;
All de time de season's changin' an' de days is gittin' cold.
An' dey's wond'rin' 'bout de metals, whethah we'll have one
    er two.
While de price o' coal is risin' an' dey's two months' rent
    dat's due.

Some folks says dat gold's de only money dat is wuff de name,
Den de othahs rise an' tell 'em dat dey ought to be ashame,
An' dat silvah is de only thing to save us f'om de powah
Of de gold-bug ragin' 'roun' an' seekin' who he may de-
    vowah.

Well, you folks kin keep on shoutin' wif yo' gold er silvah cry,
But I tell you people hams is sceerce an' fowls is roostin' high.
An' hit ain't de so't o' money dat is pesterin' my min',
But de question I want answehed's how to get at any kin'!

Jilted

Lucy done gone back on me,
    Dat's de way wif life.
Evaht'ing was movin' free,
    T'ought I had my wife.
Den some dahky comes along,
Sings my gal a little song,
Since den, evaht'ing's gone wrong,
    Evah day dey's strife.

Didn't answeh me to-day,
    W'en I called huh name,
Would you t'ink she'd ac' dat way
    W'en I ain't to blame?
Dat's de way dese women do,
W'en dey fin's a fellow true,
Den dey 'buse him thoo an' thoo;
    Well, hit's all de same.

Somep'n's wrong erbout my lung,
    An' I's glad hit's so.
Doctah says 'at I'll die young,
    Well, I wants to go!
Whut's de use o' livin' hyeah,
W'en de gal you loves so deah,
Goes back on you clean an' cleah—
    I sh'd like to know?

Chrismus on the Plantation

It was Chrismus Eve, I mind hit fu' a mighty gloomy day—
Bofe de weathah an' de people—not a one of us was gay;
Cose you'll t'ink dat's mighty funny 'twell I try to mek hit
cleah,
Fu' a da'ky's allus happy when de holidays is neah.

But we wasn't, fu' dat mo'nin' Mastah'd tol' us we mus' go,
He'd been payin' us sence freedom, but he couldn't pay
no mo';
He wa'n't nevah used to plannin' 'fo' he got so po' an' ol',
So he gwine to give up tryin', an' de homestead mus' be sol'.

I kin see him stan'in' now erpon de step ez cleah ez day,
Wid de win' a-kind o' fondlin' thoo his haih all thin an' gray;
An' I 'membah how he trimbled when he said, "It's ha'd
fu' me,
Not to mek yo' Chrismus brightah, but I 'low it wa'n't
to be."

All de women was a-cryin', an' de men, too, on de sly,
An' I noticed somep'n shinin' even in ol' Mastah's eye.
But we all stood still to listen ez ol' Ben come f'om de crowd
An' spoke up, a-try'n' to steady down his voice and mek it
loud:—

"Look hyeah, Mastah, I's been servin' you fu' lo! dese many
yeahs,
An' now, sence we's got freedom an' you's kind o' po', hit
'pears
Dat you want us all to leave you 'cause you don't t'ink you
can pay.
Ef my membry hasn't fooled me, seem dat whut I hyead
you say.

"Er in othah wo'ds, you wants us to fu'git dat you's been kin',
An' ez soon ez you is he'pless, we's to leave you hyeah behin'.
Well, ef dat's de way dis freedom ac's on people, white er
    black,
You kin jes' tell Mistah Lincum fu' to tek his freedom back.

"We gwine wo'k dis ol' plantation fu' whatevah we kin git,
Fu' I know hit did suppo't us, an' de place kin do it yit.
Now de land is yo's, de hands is ouahs, an' I reckon we'll be
    brave,
An' we'll bah ez much ez you do w'en we has to scrape an'
    save."

Ol' Mastah stood dah trimblin', but a-smilin' thoo his teahs,
An' den hit seemed jes' nachul-like, de place fah rung wid
    cheahs,
An' soon ez dey was quiet, some one sta'ted sof' an' low:
"Praise God," an' den we all jined in, "from whom all
    blessin's flow!"

Well, dey wasn't no use tryin', ouah min's was sot to stay,
An' po' ol' Mastah could n't plead ner baig, ner drive us 'way,
An' all at once, hit seemed to us, de day was bright agin,
So evahone was gay dat night, an' watched de Chrismus in.

Foolin' wid de Seasons

Seems lak folks is mighty curus
    In de way dey t'inks an' ac's.
Dey jes' spen's dey days a-mixin'
    Up de t'ings in almanacs.
Now, I min' my nex' do' neighbour,—
    He's a mighty likely man,
But he nevah t'inks o' nuffin
    'Ceptin' jes' to plot an' plan.

All de wintah he was plannin'
　　How he'd gethah sassafras
Jes' ez soon ez evah Springtime
　　Put some greenness in de grass.
An' he 'lowed a little soonah
　　He could stan' a coolah breeze
So's to mek a little money
　　F'om de sugah-watah trees.

In de summah, he'd be waihin'
　　Out de linin' of his soul,
Try 'n' ca'ci'late an' fashion
　　How he'd git his wintah coal;
An' I b'lieve he got his jedgement
　　Jes' so tuckahed out an' thinned
Dat he t'ought a robin's whistle
　　Was de whistle of de wind.

Why won't folks gin up dey plannin',
　　An' jes' be content to know
Dat dey's gittin' all dat's fu' dem
　　In de days dat come an' go?
Why won't folks quit movin' forrard?
　　Ain't hit bettah jes' to stan'
An' be satisfied wid livin'
　　In de season dat's at han'?

Hit's enough fu' me to listen
　　W'en de birds is singin' 'roun',
'Dout a-guessin' whut'll happen
　　W'en de snow is on de groun'.
In de Springtime an' de summah,
　　I lays sorrer on de she'f;
An' I knows ol' Mistah Wintah
　　Gwine to hustle fu' hisse'f.

We been put hyeah fu' a pu'pose,
   But de questun dat has riz
An' made lots o' people diffah
   Is jes' whut dat pu'pose is.
Now, accordin' to my reas'nin',
   Hyeah's de p'int whaih I's arriv,
Sence de Lawd put life into us,
   We was put hyeah fu' to live!

A Death Song

Lay me down beneaf de willers in de grass,
Whah de branch'll go a-singin' as it pass.
   An' w'en I's a-layin' low,
   I kin hyeah it as it go
Singin', "Sleep, my honey, tek yo' res' at las'."

Lay me nigh to whah hit meks a little pool,
An' de watah stan's so quiet lak an' cool,
   Whah de little birds in spring,
   Ust to come an' drink an' sing,
An' de chillen waded on dey way to school.

Let me settle w'en my shouldahs draps dey load
Nigh enough to hyeah de noises in de road;
   Fu' I t'ink de las' long res'
   Gwine to soothe my sperrit bes'
Ef I's layin' 'mong de t'ings I's allus knowed.

Jealous

Hyeah come Cæsar Higgins,
Don't he think he's fine?
Look at dem new riggin's
Ain't he tryin' to shine?
Got a standin' collar

An' a stove-pipe hat,
I'll jes' bet a dollar
Some one gin him dat.

Don't one o' you mention,
Nothin' 'bout his cloes,
Don't pay no attention,
Er let on you knows
Dat he's got 'em on him,
Why, 't'll mek him sick,
Jes go on an' sco'n him,
My, ain't dis a trick!

Look hyeah, whut's he doin'
Lookin' t' othah way?
Dat ere move's a new one,
Some one call him, "Say!"
Can't you see no pusson—
Puttin' on you' airs,
Sakes alive, you's wuss'n
Dese hyeah millionaires.

Needn't git so flighty,
Case you got dat suit.
Dem cloes ain't so mighty,—
Second hand to boot,
I's a-tryin' to spite you!
Full of jealousy!
Look hyeah, man, I'll fight you,
Don't you fool wid me!

Parted

De breeze is blowin' 'cross de bay.
    My lady, my lady;
De ship hit teks me far away,
    My lady, my lady;

Ole Mas' done sol' me down de stream;
Dey tell me 'tain't so bad's hit seem,
   My lady, my lady.

O' co'se I knows dat you'll be true,
   My lady, my lady;
But den I do' know whut to do,
   My lady, my lady;
I knowed some day we'd have to pa't,
But den hit put' nigh breaks my hea't,
   My lady, my lady.

De day is long, de night is black,
   My lady, my lady;
I know you'll wait twell I come back,
   My lady, my lady;
I'll stan' de ship, I'll stan' de chain,
But I'll come back, my darlin' Jane,
   My lady, my lady.

Jes' wait, jes' b'lieve in whut I say,
   My lady, my lady;
D' ain't nothin' dat kin keep me 'way,
   My lady, my lady;
A man's a man, an' love is love;
God knows ouah hea'ts, my little dove;
He'll he'p us f'om his th'one above,
   My lady, my lady.

A Letter

Dear Miss Lucy: I been t'inkin' dat I'd write you long fo' dis,
But dis writin' 's mighty tejous, an' you know jes' how it is.
But I's got a little lesure, so I teks my pen in han'
Fu' to let you know my feelin's since I retched dis furrin' lan'.
I's right well, I's glad to tell you (dough dis climate ain't to
   blame),

An' I hopes w'en dese lines reach you, dat dey'll fin' yo'se'f de
    same.
Cose I'se feelin kin' o' homesick—dat's ez nachul ez kin be,
W'en a feller's mo'n th'ee thousand miles across dat awful sea.
(Don't you let nobidy fool you 'bout de ocean bein' gran';
If you want to see de billers, you jes' view dem f'om de lan'.)
'Bout de people? We been t'inkin' dat all white folks was alak;
But dese Englishmen is diffunt, an' dey's curus fu' a fac'.
Fust, dey's heavier an' redder in dey make-up an' dey looks,
An' dey don't put salt nor pepper in a blessed t'ing dey cooks!
W'en dey gin you good ol' tu'nips, ca'ots, pa'snips, beets, an'
    sich,
Ef dey ain't some one to tell you, you cain't 'stinguish which is
    which.
W'en I t'ought I's eatin' chicken—you may b'lieve dis hyeah's
    a lie—
But de waiter beat me down dat I was eatin' rabbit pie.
An' dey'd t'ink dat you was crazy—jes' a reg'lar ravin' loon,
Ef you'd speak erbout a 'possum or a piece o' good ol' coon.
O, hit's mighty nice, dis trav'lin', an' I's kin' o' glad I come.
But, I reckon, now I's willin' fu' to tek my way back home.
I done see de Crystal Palace, an' I's hyeahd dey string-band
    play,
But I hasn't seen no banjos layin' nowhahs roun' dis way.
Jes' gin ol' Jim Bowles a banjo, an' he'd not go very fu',
'Fo' he'd outplayed all dese fiddlers, wif dey flourish and dey
    stir.
Evahbiddy dat I's met wif has been monst'ous kin' an' good;
But I t'ink I'd lak it better to be down in Jones's wood,
Where we ust to have sich frolics, Lucy, you an' me an' Nelse,
Dough my appetite 'ud call me, ef dey wasn't nuffin else.
I'd jes' lak to have some sweet-pertaters roasted in de skin;
I's a-longin' fu' my chittlin's an' my mustard greens ergin;
I's a-wishin' fu' some buttermilk, an' co'n braid, good an'
    brown,
An' a drap o' good ol' bourbon fu' to wash my feelin's down!
An' I's comin' back to see you jes' as ehly as I kin,
So you better not go spa'kin' wif dat wuffless scoun'el Quin!

Well, I reckon, I mus' close now; write ez soon 's dis reaches
    you;
Gi' my love to Sister Mandy an' to Uncle Isham, too.
Tell de folks I sen' 'em howdy; gin a kiss to pap an' mam;
Closin' I is, deah Miss Lucy, Still Yo' Own True-Lovin' SAM.
P.S. Ef you cain't mek out dis letter, lay it by erpon de she'f,
An' when I git home, I'll read it, darlin', to you my own se'f.

At Candle-Lightin' Time

When I come in f'om de co'n-fiel' aftah wo'kin' ha'd all day,
It's amazin' nice to fin' my suppah all erpon de way;
An' it's nice to smell de coffee bubblin' ovah in de pot,
An' it's fine to see de meat a-sizzlin' teasin'-lak an' hot.

But when suppah-time is ovah, an' de t'ings is cleahed away;
Den de happy hours dat foller are de sweetes' of de day.
When my co'ncob pipe is sta'ted, an' de smoke is drawin'
    prime,
My ole 'ooman says, "I reckon, Ike, it's candle-lightin' time."

Den de chillun snuggle up to me, an' all commence to call,
"Oh, say, daddy, now it's time to mek de shadders on de
    wall."
So I puts my han's togethah—evah daddy knows de way,—
An' de chillun snuggle closer roun' ez I begin to say:—

"Fus' thing, hyeah come Mistah Rabbit; don' you see him
    wo'k his eahs?
Huh, uh! dis mus' be a donkey,—look, how innercent he
    'pears!
Dah's de ole black swan a-swimmin'—ain't she got a' awful
    neck?
Who's dis feller dat's a-comin'? Why, dat's ole dog Tray, I
    'spec'!"

Dat's de way I run on, tryin' fu' to please 'em all I can;
Den I hollahs, "Now be keerful—dis hyeah las' 's de buga-
    man!"
An' dey runs an' hides dey faces; dey ain't skeered—dey's let-
    tin' on:
But de play ain't raaly ovah twell dat buga-man is gone.

So I jes' teks up my banjo, an' I plays a little chune,
An' you see dem haids come peepin' out to listen mighty soon.
Den my wife says, "Sich a pappy fu' to give you sich a fright!
Jes, you go to baid, an' leave him: say yo' prayers an' say
    good-night."

How Lucy Backslid

De times is mighty stirrin' 'mong de people up ouah way,
Dey 'sputin' an' dey argyin' an' fussin' night an' day;
An' all dis monst'ous trouble dat hit meks me tiahed to tell
Is 'bout dat Lucy Jackson dat was sich a mighty belle.

She was de preachah's favoured, an' he tol' de chu'ch one
    night
Dat she travelled thoo de cloud o' sin a-bearin' of a light;
But, now, I 'low he t'inkin' dat she mus' 'a' los' huh lamp,
Case Lucy done backslided an' dey trouble in de camp.

Huh daddy wants to beat huh, but huh mammy daihs him to,
Fu' she lookin' at de question f'om a 'ooman's pint o' view;
An' she say dat now she wouldn't have it diff'ent ef she could;
Dat huh darter only acted jes' lak any othah would.

Cose you know w'en women argy, dey is mighty easy led
By dey hea'ts an' don't go foolin' 'bout de reasons of de haid.
So huh mammy laid de law down (she ain' reckernizin'
    wrong),
But you got to mek erlowance fu' de cause dat go along.

Now de cause dat made Miss Lucy fu' to th'ow huh grace
    away
I's afeard won't baih no 'spection w'en hit come to jedgement
    day;
Do' de same t'ing been a-wo'kin' evah sence de worl' began,—
De 'ooman disobeyin' fu' to 'tice along a man.

Ef you 'tended de revivals which we held de wintah pas',
You kin rickolec' dat convuts was a-comin' thick an' fas';
But dey ain't no use in talkin', dey was all lef' in de lu'ch
W'en ol' Mis' Jackson's dartah foun' huh peace an' tuk de
    chu'ch.

W'y, she shouted ovah evah inch of Ebenezah's flo';
Up into de preachah's pulpit an' f'om dah down to de do';
Den she hugged an' squeezed huh mammy, an' she hugged an'
    kissed huh dad,
An' she struck out at huh sistah, people said, lak she
    was mad.

I has 'tended some revivals dat was lively in my day,
An' I's seed folks git 'uligion in mos' evah kin' o' way;
But I tell you, an' you b'lieve me dat I's speakin' true indeed,
Dat gal tuk huh 'ligion ha'dah dan de ha'dest yit I's seed.

Well, f'om dat, 't was "Sistah Jackson, won't you please do dis
    er dat?"
She mus' allus sta't de singin' w'en dey'd pass erroun' de hat,
An' hit seemed dey wasn't nuffin' in dat chu'ch dat could
    go by
'Dout sistah Lucy Jackson had a finger in de pie.

But de sayin' mighty trufeful dat hit easiah to sail
W'en de sea is ca'm an' gentle dan to weathah out a gale.
Dat's whut made dis 'ooman's trouble; ef de sto'm had kep'
    away,
She'd 'a' had enough 'uligion fu' to lasted out huh day.

Lucy went wid 'Lishy Davis, but w'en she jined chu'ch, you
    know
Dah was lots o' little places dat, of cose, she couldn't go;
An' she had to gin up dancin' an' huh singin' an' huh play.—
Now hit's nachul dat sich goin's-on 'u'd drive a man away.

So, w'en Lucy got so solemn, Ike he sta'ted fu' to go
Wid a gal who was a sinnah an' could mek a bettah show.
Lucy jes' went on to meetin' lak she didn't keer a rap,
But my 'sperunce kep' me t'inkin' dah was somep'n' gwine to
    drap.

Fu' a gal won't let 'uligion er no othah so't o' t'ing
Stop huh w'en she teks a notion dat she wants a weddin' ring.
You kin p'omise huh de blessin's of a happy aftah life
(An' hit's nice to be a angel), but she'd ravah be a wife.

So w'en Chrismus come an' mastah gin a frolic on de lawn,
Didn't 'sprise me not de littlest seein' Lucy lookin' on.
An' I seed a wa'nin' lightnin' go a-flashin' f'om huh eye
Jest ez 'Lishy an' his new gal went a-gallivantin' by.

An' dat Tildy, umph! she giggled, an' she gin huh dress a flirt
Lak de people she was passin' was ez common ez de dirt;
An' de minit she was dancin', w'y dat gal put on mo' aihs
Dan a cat a-tekin' kittens up a paih o' windin' staihs.

She could 'fo'd to show huh sma'tness, fu' she couldn't he'p
    but know
Dat wid jes' de present dancahs she was ownah of de flo';
But I t'ink she'd kin' o' cooled down ef she happened on de sly
Fu' to noticed dat 'ere lightnin' dat I seed in Lucy's eye.

An' she wouldn't been so 'stonished w'en de people gin a
    shout,
An' Lucy th'owed huh mantle back an' come a-glidin' out.
Some ahms was dah to tek huh an' she fluttahed down de flo'
Lak a feddah f'om a bedtick w'en de win' commence to blow.

Soon ez Tildy see de trouble, she jes' tu'n an' toss huh haid,
But seem lak she los' huh sperrit, all huh darin'ness was daid.
Didn't cut anothah capah nary time de blessid night;
But de othah one, hit looked lak couldn't git enough delight.

W'en you keeps a colt a-stan'nin' in de stable all along,
W'en he do git out hit's nachul he'll be pullin' mighty strong.
Ef you will tie up yo' feelin's, hyeah's de bes' advice to tek,
Look out fu' an awful loosin' w'en de string dat hol's 'em
      brek.

Lucy's mammy groaned to see huh, an' huh pappy sto'med
      an' to',
But she kep' right on a-hol'in' to de centah of de flo'.
So dey went an' ast de pastoh ef he couldn't mek huh quit,
But de tellin' of de sto'y th'owed de preachah in a fit.

Tildy Taylor chewed huh hank'cher twell she'd chewed it in a
      hole,—
All de sinnahs was rejoicin' 'cause a lamb had lef' de fol',
An' de las' I seed o' Lucy, she an' 'Lish was side an' side:
I don't blame de gal fu' dancin', an' I couldn't ef I tried.

Fu' de men dat wants to ma'y ain't a-growin' 'roun' on trees,
An' de gal dat wants to git one sholy has to try to please.
Hit's a ha'd t'ing fu' a 'ooman fu' to pray an' jes' set down,
An' to sacafice a husban' so's to try to gain a crown.

Now, I don' say she was justified in follerin' huh plan;
But aldough she los' huh 'ligion, yit she sholy got de man.
Latah on, w'en she is suttain dat de preachah's made 'em fas'
She kin jes' go back to chu'ch an' ax fu'giveness fu' de pas'!

Protest

Who say my hea't ain't true to you?
　Dey bettah heish dey mouf.
I knows I loves you thoo an' thoo
　In watah time er drouf.
I wush dese people'd stop dey talkin',
Don't mean no mo' dan chicken's squawkin':
I guess I knows which way I's walkin',
　I knows de norf f'om souf.

I does not love Elizy Brown,
　I guess I knows my min'.
You allus try to tek me down
　Wid evaht'ing you fin'.
Ef dese hyeah folks will keep on fillin'
Yo' haid wid nonsense, an' you's willin'
I bet some day dey'll be a killin'
　Somewhaih along de line.

O'cose I buys de gal ice-cream,
　Whut else I gwine to do?
I knows jes' how de t'ing 'u'd seem
　Ef I'd be sho't wid you.
On Sunday, you's at chu'ch a-shoutin',
Den all de week you go 'roun' poutin'—
I's mighty tiahed o' all dis doubtin',
　I tell you cause I's true.

FROM
WHEN MALINDY SINGS
1903

When Malindy Sings

G'way an' quit dat noise, Miss Lucy—
  Put dat music book away;
What's de use to keep on tryin'?
  Ef you practise twell you're gray,
You cain't sta't no notes a-flyin'
  Lak de ones dat rants and rings
F'om de kitchen to de big woods
  When Malindy sings.

You ain't got de nachel o'gans
  Fu' to make de soun' come right
You ain't got de tu'ns an' twistin's
  Fu' to make it sweet an' light.
Tell you one thing now, Miss Lucy,
  An' I'm tellin' you fu' true,
When hit comes to raal right singin',
  'Tain't no easy thing to do.

Easy 'nough fu' folks to hollah,
  Lookin' at de lines an' dots,
When dey ain't no one kin sence it,
  An' de chune comes in, in spots;
But fu' real melojous music,
  Dat jes' strikes yo' hea't and clings,
Jes' you stan' an' listen wif me
  When Malindy sings.

Ain't you nevah hyeahd Malindy?
  Blessed soul, tek up de cross!
Look hyeah, ain't you jokin', honey?
  Well, you don't know whut you los'.

Y' ought to hyeah dat gal a-wa'blin',
  Robins, la'ks, an' all dem things,
Heish dey moufs an' hides dey faces
  When Malindy sings.

Fiddlin' man jes' stop his fiddlin',
  Lay his fiddle on de she'f;
Mockin'-bird quit tryin' to whistle,
  'Cause he jes' so shamed hisse'f.
Folks a-playin' on de banjo
  Draps dey fingahs on de strings—
Bless yo' soul—fu'gits to move 'em,
  When Malindy sings.

She jes' spreads huh mouf and hollahs,
  "Come to Jesus," twell you hyeah
Sinnahs' tremblin' steps and voices,
  Timid-lak a-drawin' neah;
Den she tu'ns to "Rock of Ages,"
  Simply to de cross she clings,
An' you fin' yo' teahs a-drappin'
  When Malindy sings.

Who dat says dat humble praises
  Wif de Master nevah counts?
Heish yo' mouf, I hyeah dat music,
  Ez hit rises up an' mounts—
Floatin' by de hills an' valleys,
  Way above dis buryin' sod,
Ez hit makes its way in glory
  To de very gates of God!

Oh, hit's sweetah dan de music
  Of an edicated band;
An' hit's dearah dan de battle's
  Song o' triumph in de lan'.

It seems holier dan evenin'
   When de solemn chu'ch bell rings,
Ez I sit an' ca'mly listen
   While Malindy sings.

Towsah, stop dat ba'kin', hyeah me!
   Mandy, mek dat chile keep still;
Don't you hyeah de echoes callin'
   F'om de valley to de hill?
Let me listen, I can hyeah it,
   Th'oo de bresh of angels' wings,
Sof' an' sweet, "Swing Low, Sweet Chariot,"
   Ez Malindy sings.

The Colored Band

W'en de colo'ed ban' comes ma'chin' down de street,
Don't you people stan' daih starin'; lif' yo' feet!
   Ain't dey playin'? Hip, hooray!
   Stir yo' stumps an' cleah de way,
Fu' de music dat dey mekin' can't be beat.

Oh, de major man's a-swingin' of his stick,
An' de pickaninnies crowdin' roun' him thick;
   In his go'geous uniform,
   He's de lightnin' of de sto'm,
An' de little clouds erroun' look mighty slick.

You kin hyeah a fine perfo'mance w'en de white ban's sere-
   nade,
   An' dey play dey high-toned music mighty sweet,
But hit's Sousa played in ragtime, an' hit's Rastus on Parade,
   W'en de colo'ed ban' comes ma'chin' down de street.

W'en de colo'ed ban' comes ma'chin' down de street
You kin hyeah de ladies all erroun' repeat:
   "Ain't dey handsome? Ain't dey gran'?
   Ain't dey splendid? Goodness, lan'!
W'y dey's pu'fect f'om dey fo'heads to dey feet!"

An' sich steppin' to de music down de line,
'Tain't de music by itself dat meks it fine,
   Hit's de walkin', step by step,
   An' de keepin' time wid "Hep,"
Dat it mek a common ditty soun' divine.

Oh, de white ban' play hits music, an' hit's mighty good to
   hyeah,
An' it sometimes leaves a ticklin' in yo' feet;
But de hea't goes into bus'ness fu' to he'p erlong de eah,
   W'en de colo'ed ban' goes ma'chin' down de street.

The Memory of Martha

   Out in de night a sad bird moans,
      An', oh, but hit's moughty lonely;
   Times I kin sing, but mos' I groans,
      Fu' oh, but hit's moughty lonely!
   Is you sleepin' well dis evenin', Marfy, deah?
   W'en I calls you f'om de cabin, kin you hyeah?
      'Tain't de same ol' place to me,
      Nuffin' 's lak hit used to be,
   W'en I knowed dat you was allus some'ers near.

   Down by de road de shadders grows,
      An', oh, but hit's moughty lonely;
   Seem lak de ve'y moonlight knows,
      An', oh, but hit's moughty lonely!
   Does you know, I's cryin' fu' you, oh, my wife?
   Does you know dey ain't no joy no mo' in life?

An' my only t'ought is dis,
  Dat I's honin' fu' de bliss
Fu' to quit dis groun' o' worriment an' strife.

Dah on de baid my banjo lays,
  An', oh, but hit's moughty lonely;
Can't even sta't a chune o' praise,
  An', oh, but hit's moughty lonely!
Oh, hit's moughty slow a-waitin' hyeah below.
Is you watchin' fu' me, Marfy, at de do'?
  Ef you is, in spite o' sin,
  Dey'll be sho' to let me in,
W'en dey sees yo' face a-shinin', den dey'll know.

The Tryst

De night creep down erlong de lan',
  De shadders rise an' shake,
De frog is sta'tin' up his ban',
  De cricket is awake;
My wo'k is mos' nigh done, Celes',
  To-night I won't be late,
I's hu'yin' thoo my level bes',
  Wait fu' me by de gate.

De mockin'-bird 'll sen' his glee
  A-thrillin' thoo and thoo,
I know dat ol' magnolia-tree
  Is smellin' des' fu' you;
De jessamine erside de road
  Is bloomin' rich an' white,
My hea't's a-th'obbin' 'cause it knowed
  You'd wait fu' me to-night.

Hit's lonesome, ain't it, stan'in' thaih
  Wid no one nigh to talk?
But ain't dey whispahs in de aih

Erlong de gyahden walk?
Don't somep'n kin' o' call my name,
    An' say "he love you bes' "?
Hit's true, I wants to say de same,
    So wait fu' me, Celes'.

Sing somep'n fu' to pass de time,
    Outsing de mockin'-bird,
You got de music an' de rhyme,
    You beat him wid de word.
I's comin' now, my wo'k is done,
    De hour has come fu' res',
I wants to fly, but only run—
    Wait fu' me, deah Celes'.

The Boogah Man

W'en de evenin' shadders
    Come a-glidin' down,
Fallin' black an' heavy
    Ovah hill an' town,
Ef you listen keerful,
    Keerful ez you kin,
So's you boun' to notice
    Des a drappin' pin;
Den you'll hyeah a funny
    Soun' ercross de lan';
Lay low; dat's de callin'
    Of de Boogah Man!

Woo-oo, woo-oo!
    Hyeah him ez he go erlong de way;
Woo-oo, woo-oo!
    Don' you wish de night 'ud tu'n to day?

    Woo-oo, woo-oo!
      Hide yo' little peepers 'hind yo' han';
    Woo-oo, woo-oo!
      Callin' of de Boogah Man.

W'en de win's a-shiverin'
    Thoo de gloomy lane,
An' dey comes de patterin'
    Of de evenin' rain,
W'en de owl's a-hootin',
    Out daih in de wood,
Don' you wish, my honey,
    Dat you had been good?
'Tain't no use to try to
    Snuggle up to Dan;
Bless you, dat's de callin'
    Of de Boogah Man!

Ef you loves yo' mammy,
    An' you min's yo' pap,
Ef you nevah wriggles
    Outen Sukey's lap;
Ef you says yo' "Lay me"
    Evah single night
'Fo' dey tucks de kivers
    An' puts out de light,
Den de rain kin pattah
    Win' blow lak a fan,
But you needn' bothah
    'Bout de Boogah Man!

Noddin' by de Fire

Some folks t'inks hit's right an' p'opah,
    Soon ez bedtime come erroun',
Fu' to scramble to de kiver,
    Lak dey'd hyeahed de trumpet soun'.

But dese people dey all misses
      Whut I mos'ly does desiah;
Dat's de settin' roun' an' dozin',
      An' a-noddin' by de fiah.

W'en de ol' pine-knot's a-blazin',
      An' de hick'ry's crackin' free,
Den's de happy time fu' snoozin',
      It's de noddin' houah fu' me.
Den I gits my pipe a-goin',
      While I pokes de flames up highah,
An' I 'tends lak I's a-t'inkin',
      W'en I's noddin' by de fiah.

Mebbe some one comes to jine you;
      Well, dat's good, but not de bes',
Less'n dat you's kind o' lonesome,
      Er ain't honin' fu' de res'.
Den you wants to tell a sto'y,
      Er you wants to hyeah de news
Kind o' half tol', while you's stealin'
      Ev'y now an den a snooze.

W'en you's tiahed out a-hoein',
      Er a-followin' de plow,
Whut's de use of des a-fallin'
      On yo' pallet lak a cow?
W'y, de fun is all in waitin'
      In de face of all de tiah,
An' a-dozin' and a-drowsin'
      By a good ol' hick'ry fiah.

Oh, you grunts an' groans an' mumbles
      'Case yo' bones is full o' col',
Dough you feels de joy a-tricklin'
      Roun' de co'nahs of yo' soul.

An' you 'low anothah minute
    'S sho to git you wa'm an' dryah,
W'en you set up pas' yo' bedtime,
    'Ca'se you hates to leave de fiah.

Whut's de use o' downright sleep'n?
    You can't feel it while it las',
An' you git up feelin' sorry
    W'en de time fu' it is pas'.
Seem to me dat time too precious,
    An' de houahs too short entiah,
Fu' to sleep, w'en you could spen' 'em
    Des a-noddin' by de fiah.

My Sweet Brown Gal

W'en de clouds is hangin' heavy in de sky,
An' de win's's a-taihin' moughty vig'rous by,
I don' go a-sighin' all erlong de way;
I des' wo'k a-waitin' fu' de close o' day.

Case I knows w'en evenin' draps huh shadders down,
I won' care a smidgeon fu' de weathah's frown;
Let de rain go splashin', let de thundah raih,
Dey's a happy sheltah, an' I's goin' daih.

Down in my ol' cabin wa'm ez mammy's toas',
'Taters in de fiah layin' daih to roas';
No one daih to cross me, got no talkin' pal,
But I's got de comp'ny o' my sweet brown gal.

So I spen's my evenin' listenin' to huh sing,
Lak a blessid angel; how huh voice do ring!
Sweetah den a bluebird flutterin' erroun',
W'en he sees de steamin' o' de new ploughed groun'.

Den I hugs huh closah, closah to my breas'.
Needn't sing, my da'lin', tek you' hones' res'.
Does I mean Malindy, Mandy, Lize er Sal?
No, I means my fiddle—dat's my sweet brown gal!

In the Morning

'Lias! 'Lias! Bless de Lawd!
Don' you know de day's erbroad?
Ef you don' git up, you scamp,
Dey 'll be trouble in dis camp.
T'ink I gwine to let you sleep
W'ile I meks yo' boa'd an' keep?
Dat's a putty howdy-do—
Don' you hyeah me, 'Lias—you?

Bet ef I come crost dis flo'
You won' fin' no time to sno'.
Daylight all a-shinin' in
W'ile you sleep—w'y hit's a sin!
Ain't de can'le-light enough
To bu'n out widout a snuff,
But you go de mo'nin' thoo
Bu'nin' up de daylight too?

'Lias, don' you hyeah me call?
No use tu'nin' to'ds de wall;
I kin hyeah dat mattuss squeak;
Don' you hyeah me w'en I speak?
Dis hyeah clock done struck off six—
Ca'line, bring me dem ah sticks!
Oh, you down, suh; huh, you down—
Look hyeah, don' you daih to frown.

Ma'ch yo'se'f an' wash yo' face,
Don' you splattah all de place;
I got somep'n else to do,

'Sides jes' cleanin' aftah you.
Tek dat comb an' fix yo' haid—
Looks jes' lak a feddah baid.
Look hyeah, boy, I let you see
You sha'n't roll yo' eyes at me.

Come hyeah; bring me dat ah strap!
Boy, I'll whup you 'twell you drap;
You done felt yo'se'f too strong,
An' you sholy got me wrong.
Set down at dat table thaih;
Jes' you whimpah ef you daih!
Evah mo'nin' on dis place,
Seem lak I mus' lose my grace.

Fol' yo' han's an' bow yo' haid—
Wait ontwell de blessin' 's said;
"Lawd, have mussy on ouah souls—"
(Don' you daih to tech dem rolls—)
"Bless de food we gwine to eat—"
(You set still—I *see* yo' feet;
You jes' try dat trick agin!)
"Gin us peace an' joy. Amen!"

The Plantation Child's Lullaby

Wintah time hit comin'
    Stealin' thoo de night;
Wake up in the mo'nin'
    Evah t'ing is white;
Cabin lookin' lonesome
    Stannin' in de snow,
Meks you kin' o' nervous,
    W'en de win' hit blow.

Trompin' back from feedin',
  Col' an' wet an' blue,
Homespun jacket ragged,
  Win' a-blowin' thoo.
Cabin lookin' cheerful,
  Unnerneaf de do',
Yet you kin' o' keerful
  W'en de win' hit blow.

Hickory log a-blazin'
  Light a-lookin' red,
Faith o' eyes o' peepin'
  'Rom a trun'le bed,
Little feet a-patterin'
  Cleah across de flo';
Bettah had be keerful
  W'en de win' hit blow.

Suppah done an' ovah,
  Evah t'ing is still;
Listen to de snowman
  Slippin' down de hill.
Ashes on de fiah,
  Keep it wa'm but low.
What's de use o' keerin'
  Ef de win' do blow?

Smoke house full o' bacon,
  Brown an' sweet an' good;
Taters in de cellah,
  'Possum roam de wood;
Little baby snoozin'
  Des ez ef he know.
What's de use o' keerin'
  Ef de win' do blow?

Curiosity

Mammy's in de kitchen, an' de do' is shet;
All de pickaninnies climb an' tug an' sweat,
Gittin' to de winder, stickin' dah lak flies,
Evah one ermong us des all nose an' eyes.

"Whut's she cookin', Isaac?"
"Whut's she cookin', Jake?"
"Is it sweet pertaters? Is hit pie er cake?"
But we couldn't mek out even whah we stood
Whut was mammy cookin' dat could smell so good.

Mammy spread de winder, an' she frown an' frown,
How de pickaninnies come a-tumblin' down!
Den she say: "Ef you-all keeps a-peepin' in,
How I'se gwine to whup you, my! 't 'ill be a sin!
Need n' come a-sniffin' an' a-nosin' hyeah,
'Ca'se I knows my business, nevah feah."
Won't somebody tell us—how I wish dey would!—
Whut is mammy cookin' dat it smells so good?

'Twell dat steamin' kitchen brings us stealin' back,
Climbin' an' a-peepin' so's to see inside.
Whut on earf kin mammy be so sha'p to hide?
I'd des up an' tell folks w'en I knowed I could,
Ef I was a-cookin' t'ings dat smelt so good.

Mammy in de oven, an' I see huh smile;
Moufs mus' be a-wat'rin' roun' hyeah fuh a mile;
Den we almos' hollah ez we hu'ies down,
'Ca'se hit's apple dumplin's, big an' fat an' brown!
W'en de do' is opened, solemn lak an' slow,

Wisht you see us settin' all dah in a row
Innercent an' p'opah, des lak chillun should
W'en dey mammy's cookin' t'ings dat smell so good.

Opportunity

Granny's gone a-visitin',
    Seen huh git huh shawl
W'en I was a-hidin' down
    Hime de gyahden wall.
Seen huh put her bonnet on,
    Seen huh tie de strings,
An' I'se gone to dreamin' now
    'Bout dem cakes an' t'ings.

On de she'f behime de do'—
    Mussy, what a feas'!
Soon ez she gits out o' sight,
    I kin eat in peace.
I bin watchin' fu' a week
    Des fu' dis hyeah chance.
Mussy, w'en I gits in daih,
    I'll des sholy dance.

Lemon pie an' gingah-cake,
    Let me set an' t'ink—
Vinegah an' sugah, too,
    Dat'll mek a drink;
Ef dey's one t'ing dat I loves
    Mos' pu'ticlahly,
It is eatin' sweet t'ings an'
    A-drinkin' Sangaree.

Lawdy, won' po' granny raih
    W'en she see de she'f;
W'en I t'ink erbout huh face,
    I's mos' 'shamed myse'f.

Well, she gone, an hyeah I is,
　　Back behime de do'—
Look hyeah! gran' 's done 'spected me,
　　Dain't no sweets no mo'.

Evah sweet is hid erway,
　　Job des done up brown;
Pusson t'ink dat someun t'ought
　　Dey was t'eves erroun';
Dat des breaks my heart in two,
　　Oh how bad I feel!
Des to t'ink my own gramma
　　B'lieved dat I 'u'd steal!

Puttin' the Baby Away

Eight of 'em hyeah all tol' an' yet
Dese eyes o' mine is wringin' wet;
My haht's a-achin' ha'd an' so',
De way hit nevah ached befo';
My soul's a-pleadin', "Lawd, give back
Dis little lonesome baby black,
Dis one, dis las' po' he'pless one
Whose little race was too soon run."

Po' Little Jim, des fo' yeahs ol'
A-layin' down so still an' col'.
Somehow hit don' seem ha'dly faih,
To have my baby lyin' daih
Wi'dout a smile upon his face,
Wi'dout a look erbout de place;
He ust to be so full o' fun
Hit don' seem right dat all's done, done.

Des eight in all but I don' caih,
Dey wa'nt a single one to spaih;
De worl' was big, so was my haht,

An' dis hyeah baby owned hit's paht;
De house was po', dey clothes was rough,
But daih was meat an' meal enough;
An' daih was room fu' little Jim;
Oh! Lawd, what made you call fu' him?

It do seem monst'ous ha'd to-day,
To lay dis baby boy away;
I'd learned to love his teasin' smile,
He mought o' des been lef' erwhile;
You wouldn't t'ought wid all de folks,
Dat's roun' hyeah mixin' teahs an' jokes,
De Lawd u'd had de time to see
Dis chile an' tek him 'way f'om me.

But let it go, I reckon Jim,
'Ll des go right straight up to Him
Dat took him f'om his mammy's nest
An' lef' dis achin' in my breas',
An' lookin' in dat fathah's face
An' 'memberin' dis lone sorrerin' place,
He'll say, "Good Lawd, you ought to had
Do Sumpin' fu' to comfo't dad!"

Faith

I's a-gittin' weary of de way dat people do,
De folks dat's got dey 'ligion in dey fiah-place an' flue;
Dey's allus somep'n comin' so de spit'll have to turn,
An' hit tain't no p'oposition fu' to mek de hickory bu'n.
Ef de sweet pertater fails us an' de go'geous yallah yam,
We kin tek a bit o' comfo't f'om ouah sto' o' summah jam.
W'en de snow hit git to flyin', dat's de Mastah's own desiah,
De Lawd'll run de wintah an' yo' mammy'll run de fiah.

I ain' skeered because de win' hit staht to raih and blow,
I ain't bothahed w'en he come er rattlin' at de do',
Let him taih hisse'f an' shout, let him blow an' bawl,
Dat's de time de branches shek an' bresh-wood 'mence to fall.
W'en de sto'm er railin' an' de shettahs blowin' 'bout,
Dat de time de fiah-place crack hits welcome out.
Tain' my livin' business fu' to trouble ner enquiah,
De Lawd'll min' de wintah an' my mammy'll min' de fiah.

Ash-cake allus gits ez brown w'en February's hyeah
Ez it does in bakin' any othah time o' yeah.
De bacon smell ez callin'-like, de kittle rock an' sing,
De same way in de wintah dat dey do it in de spring;
Dey ain't no use in mopin' 'round an' lookin' mad an' glum
Erbout de wintah season, fu' hit's des plumb boun' to come;
An' ef it comes to runnin' t'ings I's willin' to retiah,
De Lawd'll min' de wintah an' my mammy'll min' de fiah.

The Fisher Child's Lullaby

The wind is out in its rage to-night,
   And your father is far at sea.
The rime on the window is hard and white
    But dear, you are near to me.
      Heave ho, weave low,
        Waves of the briny deep;
      Seethe low and breathe low,
        But sleep you, my little one, sleep, sleep.

The little boat rocks in the cove no more,
   But the flying sea-gulls wail;
I peer through the darkness that wraps the shore,
    For sight of a home set sail.
      Heave ho, weave low,
        Waves of the briny deep;
      Seethe low and breathe low,
        But sleep you, my little one, sleep, sleep.

Ay, lad of mine, thy father may die
  In the gale that rides the sea,
But we'll not believe it, not you and I,
  Who mind us of Galilee.
    Heave ho, weave low,
      Waves of the briny deep;
    Seethe low and breathe low,
      But sleep you, my little one, sleep, sleep.

FROM *LYRICS OF LOVE AND LAUGHTER*

1903

Joggin' Erlong

De da'kest hour, dey allus say,
Is des' befo' de dawn,
But it's moughty ha'd a-waitin'
W'ere de night goes frownin' on;
An' it's moughty ha'd a-hopin'
W'en de clouds is big an' black,
An' all de t'ings you's waited fu'
Has failed, er gone to wrack—
But des' keep on a-joggin' wid a little bit o' song,
De mo'n is allus brightah w'en de night's been long.

Dey's lots o' knocks you's got to tek
Befo' yo' journey's done,
An' dey's times w'en you'll be wishin'
Dat de weary race was run;
W'en you want to give up tryin'
An' des' float erpon de wave,
W'en you don't feel no mo' sorrer
Ez you t'ink erbout de grave—
Den, des' keep on a-joggin' wid a little bit o' song,
De mo'n is allus brightah w'en de night's been long.

De whup-lash sting a good deal mo'
De back hit 's knowed befo',
An' de burden's allus heavies'
Whaih hits weight has made a so';
Dey is times w'en tribulation
Seems to git de uppah han'
An' to whip de weary trav'lah
'Twell he ain't got stren'th to stan'—
But des' keep on a-joggin' wid a little bit o' song,
De mo'n is allus brightah w'en de night's been long.

In May

Oh to have you in May,
   To talk with you under the trees,
Dreaming throughout the day,
   Drinking the wine-like breeze,

Oh it were sweet to think
   That May should be ours again,
Hoping it not, I shrink,
   Out of the sight of men.

May brings the flowers to bloom,
   It brings the green leaves to the tree,
And the fatally sweet perfume,
   Of what you once were to me.

Dreams

What dreams we have and how they fly
Like rosy clouds across the sky;
   Of wealth, of fame, of sure success,
   Of love that comes to cheer and bless;
And how they wither, how they fade,
The waning wealth, the jilting jade—
   The fame that for a moment gleams,
   Then flies forever,—dreams, ah—dreams!

O burning doubt and long regret,
O tears with which our eyes are wet,
   Heart-throbs, heart-aches, the glut of pain,
   The somber cloud, the bitter rain,
You were not of those dreams—ah! well,

Your full fruition who can tell?
    Wealth, fame, and love, ah! love that beams
    Upon our souls, all dreams—ah! dreams.

The Dove

Out of the sunshine and out of the heat,
Out of the dust of the grimy street,
A song fluttered down in the form of a dove,
And it bore me a message, the one word—Love!

Ah, I was toiling, and oh, I was sad:
I had forgotten the way to be glad.
Now, smiles for my sadness and for my toil, rest
Since the dove fluttered down to its home in my breast!

The Valse

When to sweet music my lady is dancing
    My heart to mild frenzy her beauty inspires.
Into my face are her brown eyes a-glancing,
    And swift my whole frame thrills with tremulous fires.
Dance, lady, dance, for the moments are fleeting,
    Pause not to place yon refractory curl;
Life is for love and the night is for sweeting;
    Dreamily, joyously, circle and whirl.

Oh, how those viols are throbbing and pleading;
    A prayer is scarce needed in sound of their strain.
Surely and lightly as round you are speeding,
    You turn to confusion my heart and my brain.
Dance, lady, dance to the viol's soft calling,
    Skip it and trip it as light as the air;
Dance, for the moments like rose leaves are falling,
    Strikes, now, the clock from its place on the stair.

Now sinks the melody lower and lower,
   The weary musicians scarce seeming to play.
Ah, love, your steps now are slower and slower,
   The smile on your face is more sad and less gay.
Dance, lady, dance to the brink of our parting,
   My heart and your step must not fail to be light.
Dance! Just a turn—tho' the tear-drop be starting.
   Ah—now it is done—so—my lady, good-night!

Song

Wintah, summah, snow er shine,
   Hit's all de same to me,
Ef only I kin call you mine,
   An' keep you by my knee.

Ha'dship, frolic, grief er caih,
   Content by night an' day,
Ef only I kin see you whaih
   You wait beside de way.

Livin', dyin', smiles er teahs,
   My soul will still be free,
Ef only thoo de comin' yeahs
   You walk de worl' wid me.

Bird-song, breeze-wail, chune er moan,
   What puny t'ings dey'll be,
Ef w'en I's seemin' all erlone,
   I knows yo' hea't's wid me.

Inspiration

At the golden gate of song
Stood I, knocking all day long,
But the Angel, calm and cold,
Still refused and bade me, "Hold."

Then a breath of soft perfume,
Then a light within the gloom;
Thou, Love, camest to my side,
And the gates flew open wide.

Long I dwelt in this domain,
Knew no sorrow, grief, or pain;
Now you bid me forth and free,
Will you shut these gates on me?

When Dey 'Listed Colored Soldiers

Dey was talkin' in de cabin, dey was talkin' in de hall;
But I listened kin' o' keerless, not a-t'inkin' 'bout it all;
An' on Sunday, too, I noticed, dey was whisp'rin' mighty
    much,
Stan'in' all erroun' de roadside w'en dey let us out o' chu'ch.
But I didn't t'ink erbout it 'twell de middle of de week,
An' my 'Lias come to see me, an' somehow he couldn't speak.
Den I seed all in a minute whut he'd come to see me for;—
Dey had 'listed colo'ed sojers an' my 'Lias gwine to wah.

Oh, I hugged him, an' I kissed him, an' I baiged him not
    to go;
But he tol' me dat his conscience, hit was callin' to him so,
An' he couldn't baih to lingah w'en he had a chanst to fight
For de freedom dey had gin him an' de glory of de right.

So he kissed me, an' he lef' me, w'en I'd p'omised to be true;
An' dey put a knapsack on him, an' a coat all colo'ed blue.
So I gin him pap's ol' Bible f'om de bottom of de draw',—
W'en dey 'listed colo'ed sojers an' my 'Lias went to wah.

But I t'ought of all de weary miles dat he would have to
    tramp,
An' I couldn't be contented w'en dey tuk him to de camp.
W'y my hea't nigh broke wid grievin' 'twell I seed him on de
    street;
Den I felt lak I could go an' th'ow my body at his feet.
For his buttons was a-shinin', an' his face was shinin', too,
An' he looked so strong an' mighty in his coat o' sojer blue,
Dat I hollahed, "Step up, manny," dough my th'oat was so'
    an' raw,—
W'en dey 'listed colo'ed sojers an' my 'Lias went to wah.

Ol' Mis' cried w'en mastah lef' huh, young Miss mou'ned huh
    brothah Ned,
An' I didn't know dey feelin's is de ve'y wo'ds dey said
W'en I tol' 'em I was so'y. Dey had done gin up dey all;
But dey only seemed mo' proudah dat dey men had hyeahed
    de call.
Bofe my mastahs went in gray suits, an' I loved de Yankee
    blue,
But I t'ought dat I could sorrer for de losin' of 'em too;
But I couldn't, for I didn't know de ha'f o' whut I saw,
'Twell dey 'listed colo'ed sojers an' my 'Lias went to wah.

Mastah Jack come home all sickly; he was broke for life, dey
    said;
An' dey lef' my po' young mastah some'r's on de roadside,—
    dead.
W'en de women cried an' mou'ned 'em, I could feel it thoo
    an' thoo,
For I had a loved un fightin' in de way o' dangah, too.
Den dey tol' me dey had laid him some'r's way down souf
    to res',

Wid de flag dat he had fit for shinin' daih acrost his breas'.
Well, I cried, but den I reckon dat's whut Gawd had called
 him for,
W'en dey 'listed colo'ed sojers an' my 'Lias went to wah.

Lincoln

Hurt was the nation with a mighty wound,
And all her ways were filled with clam'rous sound.
Wailed loud the South with unremitting grief,
And wept the North that could not find relief.
Then madness joined its harshest tone to strife:
A minor note swelled in the song of life.
'Till, stirring with the love that filled his breast,
But still, unflinching at the right's behest,
Grave Lincoln came, strong handed, from afar,
The mighty Homer of the lyre of war.
'Twas he who bade the raging tempest cease,
Wrenched from his harp the harmony of peace,
Muted the strings, that made the discord,—Wrong,
And gave his spirit up in thund'rous song.
Oh mighty Master of the mighty lyre,
Earth heard and trembled at thy strains of fire:
Earth learned of thee what Heav'n already knew,
And wrote thee down among her treasured few.

To a Captious Critic

Dear critic, who my lightness so deplores,
Would I might study to be prince of bores,
Right wisely would I rule that dull estate—
But, sir, I may not, till you abdicate.

The Poet

He sang of life, serenely sweet,
   With, now and then, a deeper note.
   From some high peak, nigh yet remote,
He voiced the world's absorbing beat.

He sang of love when earth was young,
   And Love, itself, was in his lays.
   But ah, the world, it turned to praise
A jingle in a broken tongue.

A Spiritual

De 'cession's stahted on de gospel way,
   De Capting is a-drawin' nigh:
Bettah stop a-foolin' an' a-try to pray;
   Lif' up yo' haid w'en de King go by!

Oh, sinnah mou'nin' in de dusty road,
   Hyeah's de minute fu' to dry yo' eye:
Dey's a moughty One a-comin' fu' to baih yo' load;
   Lif' up yo' haid w'en de King go by!

Oh, widder weepin' by yo' husban's grave,
   Hit's bettah fu' to sing den sigh:
Hyeah come de Mastah wid de powah to save;
   Lif' up yo' haid w'en de King go by!

Oh, orphans a-weepin' lak de widder do,
   An' I wish you'd tell me why:
De Mastah is a mammy an' a pappy too;
   Lif' up yo' haid w'en de King go by!

Oh, Moses sot de sarpint in de wildahness
  W'en de chillun had commenced to die:
Some 'efused to look, but hit cuohed de res';
  Lif' up yo' haid w'en de King go by!

Bow down, bow 'way down, Bow down,
But lif' up yo' haid w'en de King go by!

W'en I Gits Home

It's moughty tiahsome layin' 'roun'
Dis sorrer-laden earfly groun',
An' oftentimes I thinks, thinks I,
'Twould be a sweet t'ing des to die,
    An' go 'long home.

Home whaih de frien's I loved 'll say,
"We've waited fu' you many a day,
Come hyeah an' res' yo'se'f, an' know
You's done wid sorrer an' wid woe,
    Now you's at home."

W'en I gits home some blessid day,
I 'lows to th'ow my caihs erway,
An' up an' down de shinin' street,
Go singin' sof' an' low an' sweet,
    W'en I gits home.

I wish de day was neah at han',
I's tiahed of dis grievin' lan',
I's tiahed of de lonely yeahs,
I want to des dry up my teahs,
    An' go 'long home.

Oh, Mastah, won't you sen' de call?
My frien's is daih, my hope, my all.
I's waitin' whaih de road is rough,
I want to hyeah you say, "Enough,
    Ol' man, come home!"

The Unsung Heroes

A song for the unsung heroes who rose in the country's need,
When the life of the land was threatened by the slaver's cruel
    greed,
For the men who came from the cornfield, who came from the
    plough and the flail,
Who rallied round when they heard the sound of the mighty
    man of the rail.

They laid them down in the valleys, they laid them down in
    the wood,
And the world looked on at the work they did, and whis-
    pered, "It is good."
They fought their way on the hillside, they fought their way in
    the glen,
And God looked down on their sinews brown, and said, "I
    have made them men."

They went to the blue lines gladly, and the blue lines took
    them in,
And the men who saw their muskets' fire thought not of their
    dusky skin.
The gray lines rose and melted beneath their scathing showers,
And they said, " 'Tis true, they have force to do, these old
    slave boys of ours."

Ah, Wagner saw their glory, and Pillow knew their blood,
That poured on a nation's altar, a sacrificial flood.
Port Hudson heard their war-cry that smote its smoke-filled
    air,
And the old free fires of their savage sires again were kindled
    there.

They laid them down where the rivers the greening valleys gem.
And the song of the thund'rous cannon was their sole re-
    quiem,
And the great smoke wreath that mingled its hue with the
    dusky cloud,
Was the flag that furled o'er a saddened world, and the sheet
    that made their shroud.

Oh, Mighty God of the Battles Who held them in Thy hand,
Who gave them strength through the whole day's length, to
    fight for their native land,
They are lying dead on the hillsides, they are lying dead on the
    plain,
And we have not fire to smite the lyre and sing them one brief
    strain.

Give, Thou, some seer the power to sing them in their might,
The men who feared the master's whip, but did not fear the
    fight;
That he may tell of their virtues as minstrels did of old,
Till the pride of face and the hate of race grow obsolete and
    cold.

A song for the unsung heroes who stood the awful test,
When the humblest host that the land could boast went forth
    to meet the best;
A song for the unsung heroes who fell on the bloody sod,
Who fought their way from night to day and struggled up
    to God.

The Pool

By the pool that I see in my dreams, dear love,
  I have sat with you time and again;
And listened beneath the dank leaves, dear love,
  To the sibilant sound of the rain.

And the pool, it is silvery bright, dear love,
  And as pure as the heart of a maid,
As sparkling and dimpling, it darkles and shines
  In the depths of the heart of the glade.

But, oh, I've a wish in my soul, dear love,
  (The wish of a dreamer, it seems,)
That I might wash free of my sins, dear love,
  In the pool that I see in my dreams.

Speakin' at de Cou't House

Dey been speakin' at de cou't house,
  An' laws-a-massy me,
'Twas de beatness kin' o' doin's
  Dat evah I did see.
Of cose I had to be dah
  In de middle o' de crowd,
An' I hallohed wid de othahs,
  W'en de speakah riz and bowed.

I was kind o' disapp'inted
  At de smallness of de man,
Case I'd allus pictered great folks
  On a mo' expansive plan;

But I t'ought I could respect him
    An' tek in de wo'ds he said,
Fu' dey sho was somp'n knowin'
    In de bald spot on his haid.

But hit did seem so't o' funny
    Aftah waitin' fu' a week
Dat de people kep' on shoutin'
    So de man des couldn't speak;
De ho'ns dey blared a little,
    Den dey let loose on de drums,—
Some one tol' me dey was playin'
    "See de conkerin' hero comes."

"Well," says I, "you all is white folks,
    But you's sutny actin' queer,
What's de use of heroes comin'
    Ef dey cain't talk w'en dey's here?"
Aftah while dey let him open,
    An' dat man he waded in,
An' he fit de wahs all ovah
    Winnin' victeries lak sin.

W'en he come down to de present,
    Den he made de feathahs fly.
He des waded in on money,
    An' he played de ta'iff high.
An' he said de colah question,
    Hit was ovah, solved, an' done,
Dat de dahky was his brothah,
    Evah blessed mothah's son.

Well he settled all de trouble
    Dat's been pesterin' de lan',
Den he set down mid de cheerin'
    An' de playin' of de ban'.

I was feelin' moughty happy
   'Twell I hyeahed somebody speak,
"Well, dat's his side of de bus'ness,
   But you wait for Jones nex' week."

Black Samson of Brandywine

"In the fight at Brandywine, Black Samson, a giant negro armed
with a scythe, sweeps his way through the red ranks. . . ."
—C. M. SKINNER s *Myths and Legends of Our Own Land.*

Gray are the pages of record,
   Dim are the volumes of eld;
Else had old Delaware told us
   More that her history held.
Told us with pride in the story,
   Honest and noble and fine,
More of the tale of my hero,
   Black Samson of Brandywine.

Sing of your chiefs and your nobles,
   Saxon and Celt and Gaul,
Breath of mine ever shall join you,
   Highly I honor them all.
Give to them all of their glory,
   But for this noble of mine,
Lend him a tithe of your tribute,
   Black Samson of Brandywine.

There in the heat of the battle,
   There in the stir of the fight,
Loomed he, an ebony giant,
   Black as the pinions of night.
Swinging his scythe like a mower
   Over a field of grain,
Needless the care of the gleaners,
   Where he had passed amain.

Straight through the human harvest,
　　Cutting a bloody swath,
Woe to you, soldier of Briton!
　　Death is abroad in his path.
Flee from the scythe of the reaper,
　　Flee while the moment is thine,
None may with safety withstand him,
　　Black Samson of Brandywine.

Was he a freeman or bondman?
　　Was he a man or a thing?
What does it matter? His brav'ry
　　Renders him royal—a king.
If he was only a chattel,
　　Honor the ransom may pay
Of the royal, the loyal black giant
　　Who fought for his country that day.

Noble and bright is the story,
　　Worthy the touch of the lyre,
Sculptor or poet should find it
　　Full of the stuff to inspire.
Beat it in brass and in copper,
　　Tell it in storied line,
So that the world may remember
　　Black Samson of Brandywine.

Douglass

Ah, Douglass, we have fall'n on evil days,
　　Such days as thou, not even thou didst know,
　　When thee, the eyes of that harsh long ago
Saw, salient, at the cross of devious ways,
And all the country heard thee with amaze.
　　Not ended then, the passionate ebb and flow,
　　The awful tide that battled to and fro;
We ride amid a tempest of dispraise.

Now, when the waves of swift dissension swarm,
    And Honor, the strong pilot, lieth stark,
Oh, for thy voice high-sounding o'er the storm,
    For thy strong arm to guide the shivering bark,
The blast-defying power of thy form,
    To give us comfort through the lonely dark.

Booker T. Washington

The word is writ that he who runs may read.
What is the passing breath of earthly fame?
But to snatch glory from the hands of blame—
That is to be, to live, to strive indeed.
A poor Virginia cabin gave the seed,
And from its dark and lowly door there came
A peer of princes in the world's acclaim,
A master spirit for the nation's need.
Strong, silent, purposeful beyond his kind,
    The mark of rugged force on brow and lip,
Straight on he goes, nor turns to look behind
    Where hot the hounds come baying at his hip;
With one idea foremost in his mind,
    Like the keen prow of some on-forging ship.

Philosophy

I been t'inkin' 'bout de preachah; whut he said de othah night,
    'Bout hit bein' people's dooty, fu' to keep dey faces bright;
How one ought to live so pleasant dat ouah tempah never riles,
    Meetin' evahbody roun' us wid ouah very nicest smiles.

Dat's all right, I ain't a-sputin' not a t'ing dat soun's lak fac',
    But you don't ketch folks a-grinnin' wid a misery in de back;
An' you don't fin' dem a-smilin' w'en dey's hongry ez kin be,
    Leastways, dat's how human natur' allus seems to 'pear
        to me.

We is mos' all putty likely fu' to have our little cares,
   An' I think we 'se doin' fus' rate w'en we jes' go long and
    bears,
Widout breakin' up ouah faces in a sickly so't o' grin,
   W'en we knows dat in ouah innards we is p'intly mad
    ez sin.

Oh dey's times fu' bein' pleasant an' fu' goin' smilin' roun',
   'Cause I don't believe in people allus totin' roun' a frown,
But it's easy 'nough to titter w'en de stew is smokin' hot,
   But hit's mighty ha'd to giggle w'en dey's nuffin' in de pot.

The Debt

This is the debt I pay
Just for one riotous day,
Years of regret and grief,
Sorrow without relief.

Pay it I will to the end—
Until the grave, my friend,
Gives me a true release—
Gives me the clasp of peace.

Slight was the thing I bought,
Small was the debt I thought,
Poor was the loan at best—
God! but the interest!

By Rugged Ways

By rugged ways and thro' the night
We struggle blindly toward the light;
And groping, stumbling, ever pray
For sight of long delaying day.
The cruel thorns beside the road

Stretch eager points our steps to goad,
And from the thickets all about
Detaining hands reach threatening out.

"Deliver us, oh, Lord," we cry,
Our hands uplifted to the sky.
No answer save the thunder's peal,
And onward, onward, still we reel.
"Oh, give us now thy guiding light;"
Our sole reply, the lightning's blight.
"Vain, vain," cries one, "in vain we call;"
But faith serene is over all.

Beside our way the streams are dried,
And famine mates us side by side.
Discouraged and reproachful eyes
Seek once again the frowning skies.
Yet shall there come, spite storm and shock,
A Moses who shall smite the rock,
Call manna from the Giver's hand,
And lead us to the promised land!

The way is dark and cold and steep,
And shapes of horror murder sleep,
And hard the unrelenting years;
But 'twixt our sighs and moans and tears,
We still can smile, we still can sing,
Despite the arduous journeying.
For faith and hope their courage lend,
And rest and light are at the end.

To the South
On Its New Slavery

Heart of the Southland, heed me pleading now,
Who bearest, unashamed, upon my brow
The long kiss of the loving tropic sun,
And yet, whose veins with thy red current run.

Borne on the bitter winds from every hand,
Strange tales are flying over all the land,
And Condemnation, with his pinions foul,
Glooms in the place where broods the midnight owl.

What art thou, that the world should point at thee,
And vaunt and chide the weakness that they see?
There was a time they were not wont to chide;
Where is thy old, uncompromising pride?

Blood-washed, thou shouldst lift up thine honored head,
White with the sorrow for thy loyal dead
Who lie on every plain, on every hill,
And whose high spirit walks the Southland still:

Whose infancy our mother's hands have nursed.
Thy manhood, gone to battle unaccursed,
Our fathers left to till th' reluctant field,
To rape the soil for what she would not yield;

Wooing for aye, the cold unam'rous sod,
Whose growth for them still meant a master's rod;
Tearing her bosom for the wealth that gave
The strength that made the toiler still a slave.

Too long we hear the deep impassioned cry
That echoes vainly to the heedless sky;
Too long, too long, the Macedonian call
Falls fainting far beyond the outward wall,

Within whose sweep, beneath the shadowing trees,
A slumbering nation takes its dangerous ease;
Too long the rumors of thy hatred go
For those who loved thee and thy children so.

Thou must arise forthwith, and strong, thou must
Throw off the smirching of this baser dust,
Lay by the practice of this later creed,
And be thine honest self again indeed.

There was a time when even slavery's chain
Held in some joys to alternate with pain,
Some little light to give the night relief,
Some little smiles to take the place of grief.

There was a time when, jocund as the day,
The toiler hoed his row and sung his lay,
Found something gleeful in the very air,
And solace for his toiling everywhere.

Now all is changed, within the rude stockade,
A bondsman whom the greed of men has made
Almost too brutish to deplore his plight,
Toils hopeless on from joyless morn till night.

For him no more the cabin's quiet rest,
The homely joys that gave to labor zest;
No more for him the merry banjo's sound,
Nor trip of lightsome dances footing round.

For him no more the lamp shall glow at eve,
Nor chubby children pluck him by the sleeve;
No more for him the master's eyes be bright,—
He has nor freedom's nor a slave's delight.

What, was it all for naught, those awful years
That drenched a groaning land with blood and tears?
Was it to leave this sly convenient hell,
That brother fighting his own brother fell?

When that great struggle held the world in awe,
And all the nations blanched at what they saw,
Did Sanctioned Slavery bow its conquered head
That this unsanctioned crime might rise instead?

Is it for this we all have felt the flame,—
This newer bondage and this deeper shame?
Nay, not for this, a nation's heroes bled,
And North and South with tears beheld their dead.

Oh, Mother South, hast thou forgot thy ways,
Forgot the glory of thine ancient days,
Forgot the honor that once made thee great,
And stooped to this unhallowed estate?

It cannot last, thou wilt come forth in might,
A warrior queen full armored for the fight;
And thou wilt take, e'en with thy spear in rest,
Thy dusky children to thy saving breast.

Till then, no more, no more the gladsome song,
Strike only deeper chords, the notes of wrong;
Till then, the sigh, the tear, the oath, the moan,
Till thou, oh, South, and thine, come to thine own.

The Haunted Oak

Pray why are you so bare, so bare,
  Oh, bough of the old oak-tree;
And why, when I go through the shade you throw,
  Runs a shudder over me?

My leaves were green as the best, I trow,
  And sap ran free in my veins,
But I saw in the moonlight dim and weird
  A guiltless victim's pains.

I bent me down to hear his sigh;
  I shook with his gurgling moan,
And I trembled sore when they rode away,
  And left him here alone.

They'd charged him with the old, old crime,
  And set him fast in jail:
Oh, why does the dog howl all night long,
  And why does the night wind wail?

He prayed his prayer and he swore his oath,
  And he raised his hand to the sky;
But the beat of hoofs smote on his ear,
  And the steady tread drew nigh.

Who is it rides by night, by night,
  Over the moonlit road?
And what is the spur that keeps the pace,
  What is the galling goad?

And now they beat at the prison door,
   "Ho, keeper, do not stay!
We are friends of him whom you hold within,
   And we fain would take him away

"From those who ride fast on our heels
   With mind to do him wrong;
They have no care for his innocence,
   And the rope they bear is long."

They have fooled the jailer with lying words,
   They have fooled the man with lies;
The bolts unbar, the locks are drawn,
   And the great door open flies.

Now they have taken him from the jail,
   And hard and fast they ride,
And the leader laughs low down in his throat,
   As they halt my trunk beside.

Oh, the judge, he wore a mask of black,
   And the doctor one of white,
And the minister, with his oldest son,
   Was curiously bedight.

Oh, foolish man, why weep you now?
   'Tis but a little space,
And the time will come when these shall dread
   The mem'ry of your face.

I feel the rope against my bark,
   And the weight of him in my grain,
I feel in the throe of his final woe
   The touch of my own last pain.

And never more shall leaves come forth
  On a bough that bears the ban;
I am burned with dread, I am dried and dead,
  From the curse of a guiltless man.

And ever the judge rides by, rides by,
  And goes to hunt the deer,
And ever another rides his soul
  In the guise of a mortal fear.

And ever the man he rides me hard,
  And never a night stays he;
For I feel his curse as a haunted bough,
  On the trunk of a haunted tree.

Weltschmertz

You ask why I am sad to-day,
I have no cares, no griefs, you say?
Ah, yes, 'tis true, I have no grief—
But—is there not the falling leaf?

The bare tree there is mourning left
With all of autumn's gray bereft;
It is not what has happened me,
Think of the bare, dismantled tree.

The birds go South along the sky,
I hear their lingering, long good-bye.
Who goes reluctant from my breast?
And yet—the lone and windswept nest.

The mourning, pale-flowered hearse goes by,
Why does a tear come to my eye?
Is it the March rain blowing wild?
I have no dead, I know no child.

I am no widow by the bier
Of him I held supremely dear.
I have not seen the choicest one
Sink down as sinks the westering sun.

Faith unto faith have I beheld,
For me, few solemn notes have swelled;
Love beckoned me out to the dawn,
And happily I followed on.

And yet my heart goes out to them
Whose sorrow is their diadem;
The falling leaf, the crying bird,
The voice to be, all lost, unheard—

Not mine, not mine, and yet too much
The thrilling power of human touch,
While all the world looks on and scorns
I wear another's crown of thorns.

Count me a priest who understands
The glorious pain of nail-pierced hands;
Count me a comrade of the thief
Hot driven into late belief.

Oh, mother's tear, oh, father's sigh,
Oh, mourning sweetheart's last good-bye,
I yet have known no mourning save
Beside some brother's brother's grave.

Robert Gould Shaw

Why was it that the thunder voice of Fate
    Should call thee, studious, from the classic groves,
    Where calm-eyed Pallas with still footstep roves,
And charge thee seek the turmoil of the state?
What bade thee hear the voice and rise elate,

Leave home and kindred and thy spicy loaves,
To lead th' unlettered and despised droves
To manhood's home and thunder at the gate?

Far better the slow blaze of Learning's light,
The cool and quiet of her dearer fane,
Than this hot terror of a hopeless fight,
This cold endurance of the final pain,—
Since thou and those who with thee died for right
Have died, the Present teaches, but in vain!

A Love Song

Ah, love, my love is like a cry in the night,
A long, loud cry to the empty sky,
The cry of a man alone in the desert,
With hands uplifted, with parching lips,

Oh, rescue me, rescue me,
Thy form to mine arms,
The dew of thy lips to my mouth,
Dost thou hear me?—my call thro' the night?

Darling, I hear thee and answer,
Thy fountain am I,
All of the love of my soul will I bring to thee,
All of the pains of my being shall wring to thee,
Deep and forever the song of my loving shall sing to thee,
Ever and ever thro' day and thro' night shall I cling to thee.
Hearest thou the answer?
Darling, I come, I come.

A Negro Love Song

Seen my lady home las' night,
   Jump back, honey, jump back.
Hel' huh han' an' sque'z it tight,
   Jump back, honey, jump back.
Hyeahd huh sigh a little sigh,
Seen a light gleam f'om huh eye,
An' a smile go flittin' by—
   Jump back, honey, jump back.

Hyeahd de win' blow thoo de pine,
   Jump back, honey, jump back.
Mockin'-bird was singin' fine,
   Jump back, honey, jump back.
An' my hea't was beatin' so,
When I reached my lady's do',
Dat I couldn't ba' to go—
   Jump back, honey, jump back.

Put my ahm aroun' huh wais',
   Jump back, honey, jump back.
Raised huh lips an' took a tase,
   Jump back, honey, jump back.
Love me, honey, love me true?
Love me well ez I love you?
An' she answe'd, " 'Cose I do"—
   Jump back, honey, jump back.

The Fount of Tears

All hot and grimy from the road,
    Dust gray from arduous years,
I sat me down and eased my load
    Beside the Fount of Tears.

The waters sparkled to my eye,
    Calm, crystal-like, and cool,
And breathing there a restful sigh,
    I bent me to the pool.

When, lo! a voice cried: "Pilgrim, rise,
    Harsh tho' the sentence be,
And on to other lands and skies—
    This fount is not for thee.

"Pass on, but calm thy needless fears,
    Some may not love or sin,
An angel guards the Fount of Tears;
    All may not bathe therein."

Then with my burden on my back
    I turned to gaze awhile,
First at the uninviting track,
    Then at the water's smile.

And so I go upon my way,
    Thro'out the sultry years,
But pause no more, by night, by day,
    Beside the Fount of Tears.

At the Tavern

A lilt and a swing,
   And a ditty to sing,
Or ever the night grow old;
   The wine is within,
   And I'm sure 'twere a sin
For a soldier to choose to be cold, my dear,
For a soldier to choose to be cold.

We're right for a spell,
   But the fever is—well,
No thing to be braved, at least;
   So bring me the wine;
   No low fever in mine,
For a drink is more kind than a priest, my dear,
For a drink is more kind than a priest.

FROM *LI'L' GAL*

1904

Li'l' Gal

Oh, de weathah it is balmy an' de breeze is sighin' low.
  Li'l' gal,
An' de mockin' bird is singin' in de locus' by de do',
  Li'l' gal;
Dere's a hummin' an' a bummin' in de lan' f'om eas' to wes',
I's a-sighin' fu' you, honey, an' I nevah know no res'.
Fu' dey's lots o' trouble brewin' an' a-stewin' in my breas',
  Li'l' gal.

Whut's de mattah wid de weathah, whut's de mattah wid de
  breeze,
  Li'l' gal?
Whut's de mattah wid de locus' dat's a-singin' in de trees,
  Li'l' gal?
W'y dey knows dey ladies love 'em, an' dey knows dey love
  'em true,
An' dey love 'em back, I reckon, des' lak I's a-lovin' you;
Dat's de reason dey's a-weavin' an' a-sighin', thoo an' thoo,
  Li'l' gal.

Don't you let no da'ky fool you 'cause de clo'es he waihs is
  fine,
  Li'l' gal.
Dey's a hones' hea't a-beatin' unnerneaf dese rags o' mine,
  Li'l' gal.
C'ose dey ain' no use in mockin' whut de birds an'
  weathah do,
But I's so'y I cain't 'spress it w'en I knows I loves you true,
Dat's de reason I's a-sighin' an' a-singin now fu' you,
  Li'l' gal.

A Plea

Treat me nice, Miss Mandy Jane,
    Treat me nice.
Dough my love has tu'ned my brain,
    Treat me nice.
I ain't done a t'ing to shame,
Lovahs all ac's jes' de same:
Don't you know we ain't to blame?
    Treat me nice!

Cose I know I 's talkin' wild;
    Treat me nice;
I cain't talk no bettah, child,
    Treat me nice;
Whut a pusson gwine to do,
W'en he come a-cou'tin' you
All a-trimblin' thoo and thoo?
    Please be nice.

Reckon I mus' go de paf
    Othahs do:
Lovahs lingah, ladies laff;
    Mebbe you
Do' mean all the things you say,
An' pu'haps some latah day
W'en I baig you ha'd, you may
    Treat me nice!

Soliloquy of a Turkey

Dey's a so't o' threatenin' feelin' in de blowin' of de breeze,
    An' I's feelin' kin' o' squeamish in de night;
I's a-walkin' 'roun' a-lookin' at de diffunt style o' trees,

An' a-measurin' dey thickness an' dey height.
Fu' dey's somep'n mighty 'spicious in de looks de da'kies give,
  Ez dey pass me an' my fambly on de groun,'
So it 'curs to me dat lakly, ef I caihs to try an' live,
  It concehns me fu' to 'mence to look erroun'.

Dey's a cu'ious kin' o' shivah runnin' up an' down my back,
  An' I feel my feddahs rufflin' all de day,
An' my laigs commence to trimble evah blessid step I mek;
  W'en I sees a ax, I tu'ns my head away.
Folks is go'gin' me wid goodies, an' dey's treatin' me wid caih,
  An' I's fat in spite of all dat I kin do.
I's mistrus'ful of de kin'ness dat's erroun' me evahwhaih,
  Fu' it's jes' too good, an' frequent, to be true.

Snow's a-fallin' on de medders, all erroun' me now is white,
  But I's still kep' on a-roostin' on de fence;
Isham comes an' feels my breas' bone, an' he hefted me las'
    night,
  An' he's gone erroun' a-grinnin' evah sence.
'Tain't de snow dat meks me shivah; 't ain't de col' dat meks
    me shake;
  'Tain't de wintah-time itse'f dat's 'fectin' me;
But I t'ink de time is comin', an' I'd bettah mek a break,
  Fu' to set wid Mistah Possum in his tree.

W'en you hyeah de da'kies singin', an' de quahtahs all is gay,
  'Tain't de time fu' birds lak me to be erroun';
W'en de hick'ry chips is flyin', an' de log's been ca'ied erway,
  Den hit's dang'ous to be roostin' nigh de groun'.

Grin on, Isham! Sing on, da'kies! But I flop my wings an' go
  Fu' de sheltah of de ve'y highest tree,
Fu' dey's too much close ertention—an' dey's too much fallin'
    snow—
  An' it's too nigh Chris'mus mo'nin' now fu' me.

When Sam'l Sings

Hyeah dat singin' in de medders
    Whaih de folks is mekin' hay?
Wo'k is pretty middlin' heavy
    Fu' a man to be so gay.
You kin tell dey's somep'n special
    F'om de canter o' de song;
Somep'n sholy pleasin' Sam'l,
    W'en he singin' all day long.

Hyeahd him wa'blin' 'way dis mo'nin'
    'Fo' 'twas light enough to see.
Seem lak music in de evenin'
    Allus good enough fu' me.
But dat man commenced to hollah
    'Fo' he'd even washed his face;
Would you b'lieve, de scan'lous rascal
    Woke de birds erroun' de place?

Sam'l took a trip a-Sad'day;
    Dressed hisse'f in all he had,
Tuk a cane an' went a-strollin',
    Lookin' mighty pleased an' glad.
Some folks don' know whut de mattah,
    But I do, you bet yo' life;
Sam'l smilin' an' a-singin'
    'Case he been to see his wife.

She live on de fu' plantation,
    Twenty miles erway er so;
But huh man is mighty happy
    W'en he git de chanst to go.

Walkin' allus ain' de nices'—
  Mo'nin' fin's him on de way—
But he allus comes back smilin',
  Lak his pleasure was his pay.

Den he do a heap o' talkin',
  Do' he mos'ly kin' o' still,
But de wo'ds, dey gits to runnin'
  Lak de watah fu' a mill.
"Whut's de use o' havin' trouble,
  Whut's de use o' havin' strife?"
Dat's de way dis Sam'l preaches
  W'en he been to see his wife.

An' I reckon I git jealous,
  Fu' I laff an' joke an' sco'n,
An' I say, "Oh, go on, Sam'l,
  Des go on, an' blow yo' ho'n."
But I know dis comin' Sad'day,
  Dey'll be brighter days in life;
An' I'll be ez glad ez Sam'l
  W'en I go to see my wife.

FROM *LYRICS OF SUNSHINE AND SHADOW*

1905

A Boy's Summer Song

'Tis fine to play
In the fragrant hay,
And romp on the golden load;
To ride old Jack
To the barn and back,
Or tramp by a shady road.
To pause and drink,
At a mossy brink;
Ah, that is the best of joy,
And so I say
On a summer's day,
What's so fine as being a boy?
Ha, Ha!

With line and hook
By a babbling brook,
The fisherman's sport we ply;
And list the song
Of the feathered throng
That flit in the branches nigh.
At last we strip
For a quiet dip;
Ah, that is the best of joy.
For this I say
On a summer's day,
What's so fine as being a boy?
Ha, Ha!

The Sand-Man

I know a man
With face of tan,
But who is ever kind;
Whom girls and boys
Leaves games and toys
Each eventide to find.

When day grows dim,
They watch for him,
He comes to place his claim;
He wears the crown
Of Dreaming-town;
The sand-man is his name.

When sparkling eyes
Troop sleepywise
And busy lips grow dumb;
When little heads
Nod toward the beds,
We know the sand-man's come.

Johnny Speaks

The sand-man he's a jolly old fellow,
His face is kind and his voice is mellow,
But he makes your eyelids as heavy as lead,
And then you got to go off to bed;
I don't think I like the sand-man.

But I've been playing this live-long day;
It does make a fellow so tired to play!
Oh, my, I'm a-yawning right here before ma,
I'm the sleepiest fellow that ever you saw.
   I think I do like the sand-man.

Scamp

Ain't it nice to have a mammy
   W'en you kin' o' tiahed out
Wid a-playin' in de meddah,
   An' a-runnin' roun' about
Till hit's made you mighty hongry,
   An' yo' nose hit gits to know
What de smell means dat's a-comin'
   F'om de open cabin do'?
     She wash yo' face,
     An' mek yo' place,
   You's hongry as a tramp;
Den hit's eat you suppah right away,
   You sta'vin' little scamp.

W'en you's full o' braid an' bacon,
   An' dey ain't no mo' to eat,
An' de lasses dat's a-stickin'
   On yo' face ta'se kin' o' sweet,
Don' you t'ink hit's kin' o' pleasin'
   Fu' to have som'body neah
Dat'll wipe yo' han's an' kiss you
   Fo' dey lif' you f'om you' cheah?
     To smile so sweet,
     An' wash yo' feet,
   An' leave 'em co'l an' damp;
Den hit's come let me undress you, now
   You lazy little scamp.

Don' yo' eyes git awful heavy,
  An' yo' lip git awful slack,
Ain't dey som'p'n' kin' o' weaknin'
  In de backbone of yo' back?
Don' yo' knees feel kin' o' trimbly,
  An' yo' head go bobbin' roun',
W'en you says yo' "Now I lay me,"
  An' is sno'in on de "down"?
    She kiss yo' nose,
    She kiss yo' toes,
   An' den tu'n out de lamp,
Den hit's creep into yo' trunnel baid,
  You sleepy little scamp.

A *Christmas Folksong*

De win' is blowin' wahmah,
  An hit's blowin' f'om de bay;
Dey's a so't o' mist a-risin'
  All erlong de meddah way;
Dey ain't a hint o' frostin'
  On de groun' ner in de sky,
An' dey ain't no use in hopin'
  Dat de snow'll 'mence to fly.
    It's goin' to be a green Christmas,
     An' sad de day fu' me.
   I wish dis was de las' one
    Dat evah I should see.

Dey's dancin' in de cabin,
  Dey's spahkin' by de tree;
But dancin' times an' spahkin'
  Are all done pas' fur me.
Dey's feastin' in de big house,
  Wid all de windahs wide—
Is dat de way fu' people
  To meet de Christmas-tide?

It's goin' to be a green Christmas,
  No mattah what you say.
Dey's us dat will remembah
  An' grieve de comin' day.

Dey's des a bref o' dampness
  A-clingin' to my cheek;
De aih's been dahk an' heavy
  An' threatenin' fu' a week,
But not wid signs o' wintah,
  Dough wintah'd seem so deah—
De wintah's out o' season,
  An' Christmas eve is heah.
    It's goin' to be a green Christmas,
      An' oh, how sad de day!
    Go ax de hongry chu'chya'd,
      An' see what hit will say.

Dey's Allen on de hillside,
  An' Marfy in de plain;
Fu' Christmas was like springtime,
  An' come wid sun an' rain.
Dey's Ca'line, John, an' Susie,
  Wid only dis one lef':
An' now de curse is comin'
  Wid murder in hits bref.
    It's goin' to be a green Christmas—
      Des hyeah my words an' see:
    Befo' de summah beckons
      Dey's many'll weep wid me.

The Farm Child's Lullaby

Oh, the little bird is rocking in the cradle of the wind,
  And it's bye, my little wee one, bye;
The harvest all is gathered and the pippins all are binned;
  Bye, my little wee one, bye;

The little rabbit's hiding in the golden shock of corn,
The thrifty squirrel's laughing bunny's idleness to scorn;
You are smiling with the angels in your slumber, smile till
    morn;
    So it's bye, my little wee one, bye.

There'll be plenty in the cellar, there'll be plenty on the shelf;
    Bye, my little wee one, bye;
There'll be goodly store of sweetings for a dainty little elf;
    Bye, my little wee one, bye.
The snow may be a-flying o'er the meadow and the hill,
The ice has checked the chatter of the little laughing rill,
But in your cosey cradle you are warm and happy still;
    So bye, my little wee one, bye.

Why, the Bob White thinks the snowflake is a brother to his
    song;
    Bye, my little wee one, bye;
And the chimney sings the sweeter when the wind is blowing
    strong;
    Bye, my little wee one, bye;
The granary's overflowing, full is cellar, crib, and bin,
The wood has paid its tribute and the ax has ceased its din;
The winter may not harm you when you're sheltered safe
    within;
    So bye, my little wee one, bye.

Hope

De dog go howlin' 'long de road,
    De night come shiverin' down;
My back is tiahed of its load,
    I cain't be fu' f'om town.
No mattah ef de way is long,
My haht is swellin' wid a song,
    No mattah 'bout de frownin' skies,
    I'll soon be home to see my Lize.

My shadder staggah on de way,
    It's monstous col' to-night;
But I kin hyeah my honey say
    "W'y bless me if de sight
O' you ain't good fu' my so' eyes."
(Dat talk's dis lak my lady Lize)
    I's so'y case de way was long
    But Lawd you bring me love an' song.

No mattah ef de way is long,
    An' ef I trimbles so'
I knows de fiah's burnin' strong,
    Behime my Lizy's do'.
An' daih my res' an' joy shell be,
Whaih my ol' wife's awaitin' me—
    Why what I keer fu's stingin' blas',
    I see huh windah light at las'.

The Awakening

I did not know that life could be so sweet,
I did not know the hours could speed so fleet,
Till I knew you, and life was sweet again.
The days grew brief with love and lack of pain—

I was a slave a few short days ago,
The powers of Kings and Princes now I know;
I would not be again in bondage, save
I had your smile, the liberty I crave.

A Musical

Outside the rain upon the street,
    The sky all grim of hue,
Inside, the music-painful sweet,
    And yet I heard but you.

As is a thrilling violin,
    So is your voice to me,
And still above the other strains,
    It sang in ecstasy.

Twell de Night Is Pas'

All de night long twell de moon goes down,
    Lovin' I set at huh feet,
Den fu' de long jou'ney back f'om de town,
    Ha'd, but de dreams mek it sweet.

All de night long twell de break of de day,
    Dreamin' agin in my sleep,
Mandy comes drivin' my sorrers away,
    Axin' me, "Wha' fu' you weep?"

All de day long twell de sun goes down,
    Smilin', I ben' to my hoe,
Fu' dough de weddah git nasty an' frown,
    One place I know I kin go.

All my life long twell de night has pas'
    Let de wo'k come ez it will,
So dat I fin' you, my honey, at las',
    Somewhaih des ovah de hill.

Compensation

Because I had loved so deeply,
    Because I had loved so long,
God in His great compassion
    Gave me the gift of song.

Because I have loved so vainly,
  And sung with such faltering breath,
The Master in infinite mercy
  Offers the boon of Death.

Anchored

If thro' the sea of night which here surrounds me,
  I could swim out beyond the farthest star,
Break every barrier of circumstance that bounds me,
  And greet the Sun of sweeter life afar,

Tho' near you there is passion, grief, and sorrow,
  And out there rest and joy and peace and all,
I should renounce that beckoning for to-morrow,
  I could not choose to go beyond your call.

Yesterday and To-morrow

Yesterday I held your hand,
  Reverently I pressed it,
And its gentle yieldingness
  From my soul I blessed it.

But to-day I sit alone,
  Sad and sore repining;
Must our gold forever know
  Flames for the refining?

Yesterday I walked with you,
  Could a day be sweeter?
Life was all a lyric song
  Set to tricksy meter.

Ah, to-day is like a dirge,—
Place my arms around you,
Let me feel the same dear joy
As when first I found you.

Let me once retrace my steps,
From these roads unpleasant,
Let my heart and mind and soul
All ignore the present.

Yesterday the iron seared
And to-day means sorrow.
Pause, my soul, arise, arise,
Look where gleams the morrow.

At Sunset Time

Adown the west a golden glow
    Sinks burning in the sea,
And all the dreams of long ago
    Come flooding back to me.
The past has writ a story strange
    Upon my aching heart,
But time has wrought a subtle change,
    My wounds have ceased to smart.

No more the quick delight of youth,
    No more the sudden pain,
I look no more for trust or truth
    Where greed may compass gain.
What, was it I who bared my heart
    Through unrelenting years,
And knew the sting of misery's dart,
    The tang of sorrow's tears?

'Tis better now, I do not weep,
　　I do not laugh nor care;
My soul and spirit half asleep
　　Drift aimless everywhere.
We float upon a sluggish stream,
　　We ride no rapids mad,
While life is all a tempered dream
　　And every joy half sad.

At Loafing-Holt

Since I left the city's heat
For this sylvan, cool retreat,
High upon the hill-side here
Where the air is clean and clear,
I have lost the urban ways.
Mine are calm and tranquil days,
Sloping lawns of green are mine,
Clustered treasures of the vine;
Long forgotten plants I know,
Where the best wild berries grow,
Where the greens and grasses sprout,
When the elders blossom out.
Now I am grown weather-wise
With the lore of winds and skies.
Mine the song whose soft refrain
Is the sigh of summer rain.
Seek you where the woods are cool,
Would you know the shady pool
Where, throughout the lazy day,
Speckled beauties drowse or play?
Would you find in rest or peace
Sorrow's permanent release?—
Leave the city, grim and gray,
Come with me, ah, come away.
Do you fear the winter chill,
Deeps of snow upon the hill?

'Tis a mantle, kind and warm,
Shielding tender shoots from harm.
Do you dread the ice-clad streams,—
They are mirrors for your dreams.
Here's a rouse, when summer's past
To the raging winter's blast.
Let him roar and let him rout,
We are armored for the bout.
How the logs are glowing, see!
Who sings louder, they or he?
Could the city be more gay?
Burn your bridges! Come away!

When a Feller's Itchin' to Be Spanked

W'en us fellers stomp around, makin' lots o' noise,
Gramma says, "There's certain times come to little boys
W'en they need a shingle or the soft side of a plank;"
She says "we're a-itchin' for a right good spank."
    An' she says, "Now thes you wait,
    It's a-comin'—soon or late,
W'en a feller's itchin' fer a spank."

W'en a feller's out o' school, you know how he feels,
Gramma says we wriggle 'roun' like a lot o' eels.
W'y it's like a man that's thes home from out o' jail.
What's the use o' scoldin' if we pull Tray's tail?
    Gramma says, tho', "Thes you wait,
    It's a-comin'—soon or late,
You'se the boys that's itchin' to be spanked."

Cats is funny creatures an' I like to make 'em yowl,
Gramma alwus looks at me with a awful scowl
An' she says, "Young gentlemen, mamma should be thanked

Ef you'd get your knickerbockers right well spanked."
  An' she says, "Now thes you wait,
    It's a-comin'—soon or late,"
W'en a feller's itchin' to be spanked.

Ef you fin' the days is gettin' awful hot in school
An' you know a swimmin' place where it's nice and cool,
Er you know a cat-fish hole brimmin' full o' fish,
Whose a-goin' to set around school and wish?
    'Tain't no use to hide your bait,
    It's a-comin,—soon or late,
W'en a feller's itchin' to be spanked.

Ol' folks know most ever'thing 'bout the world, I guess,
Gramma does, we wish she knowed thes a little less,
But I alwus kind o' think it 'ud be as well
    Ef they wouldn't alwus have to up an' tell;
    We kids wish 'at they'd thes wait,
    It's a-comin'—soon or late,
W'en a feller's itchin' to be spanked.

A Love Letter

Oh, I des received a letter f'om de sweetest little gal;
        Oh, my; oh, my.
She's my lovely little sweetheart an' her name is Sal:
        Oh, my; oh, my.
She writes me dat she loves me an' she loves me true,
She wonders ef I'll tell huh dat I loves huh, too;
An' my heaht's so full o' music dat I do' know what to do;
        Oh, my; oh, my.

I got a man to read it an' he read it fine;
        Oh, my; oh, my.
Dey ain' no use denying dat her love is mine;
        Oh, my; oh, my.
But hyeah's de t'ing dat's puttin' me in such a awful plight,

I t'ink of huh at mornin' an' I dream of huh at night;
But how's I gwine to cou't huh w'en I do' know how to write?
    Oh, my; oh, my.

My heaht is bubblin' ovah wid de t'ings I want to say;
    Oh, my; oh, my.
An' dey's lots of folks to copy what I tell 'em fu' de pay;
    Oh, my; oh, my.
But dey's t'ings dat I's a-t'inkin' dat is only fu' huh ears,
An' I couldn't lu'n to write 'em ef I took a dozen years;
So to go down daih an' tell huh is de only way, it 'pears;
    Oh, my; oh, my.

Trouble in de Kitchen

Dey was oncet a awful quoil 'twixt de skillet an' de pot;
De pot was des a-bilin' an' de skillet sho' was hot.
Dey slurred each othah's colah an' dey called each othah
    names,
W'ile de coal-oil can des gu-gled, po'in oil erpon de flames.

De pot, hit called de skillet des a flat, disfiggered t'ing,
An' de skillet 'plied dat all de pot could do was set an' sing,
An' he 'lowed dat dey was 'lusions dat he wouldn't stoop
    to mek
'Case he reckernize his juty, an' he had too much at stake.

Well, at dis de pot biled ovah, case his tempah gittin' highah,
An' de skillet got to sputterin', den de fat was in de fiah.
Mistah fiah lay daih smokin' an' a-t'inkin' to hisse'f,
W'ile de peppah-box us nudgin' of de gingah on de she'f.

Den dey all des lef' hit to 'im, 'bout de trouble an' de talk;
An' howevah he decided, w'y dey bofe 'u'd walk de chalk;
But de fiah uz so 'sgusted how dey quoil an' dey shout
Dat he cooled 'em off, I reckon, w'en he puffed an' des
    went out.

The Quilting

Dolly sits a-quilting by her mother, stitch by stitch,
Gracious, how my pulses throb, how my fingers itch,
While I note her dainty waist and her slender hand,
As she matches this and that, she stitches strand by strand.
And I long to tell her Life's a quilt and I'm a patch;
Love will do the stitching if she'll only be my match.

Forever

I had not known before
  Forever was so long a word.
The slow stroke of the clock of time
  I had not heard.

'Tis hard to learn so late;
  It seems no sad heart really learns,
But hopes and trusts and doubts and fears,
  And bleeds and burns.

The night is not all dark,
  Nor is the day all it seems,
But each may bring me this relief—
  My dreams and dreams.

I had not known before
  That Never was so sad a word,
So wrap me in forgetfulness—
  I have not heard.

Parted

She wrapped her soul in a lace of lies,
    With a prime deceit to pin it;
And I thought I was gaining a fearsome prize,
    So I staked my soul to win it.

We wed and parted on her complaint,
    And both were a bit of barter,
Tho' I'll confess that I'm no saint,
    I'll swear that she's no martyr.

Christmas

Step wid de banjo an' glide wid de fiddle,
    Dis ain' no time fu' to pottah an' piddle;
Fu' Christmas is comin', it's right on de way,
    An' dey's houahs to dance 'fo' de break o' de day.

What if de win' is taihin' an' whistlin'?
    Look at dat fiah how hit's spittin' an' bristlin'!
Heat in de ashes an' heat in de cindahs,
    Ol' mistah Fros' kin des look thoo de windahs.

Heat up de toddy an' pas' de wa'm glasses,
    Don' stop to shivah at blowin's an' blas'es,
Keep on de kittle an' keep it a-hummin',
    Eat all an' drink all, dey's lots mo' a-comin'.
Look hyeah, Maria, don't open dat oven,
    Want all dese people a-pushin' an' shovin'?

Res' f'om de dance? Yes, you done cotch dat odah,
    Mammy done cotch it, an' law! hit nigh flo'd huh;
'Possum is monst'ous fu' mekin' folks fin' it!
    Come, draw yo' cheers up, I's sho' I do' min' it.
Eat up dem critters, you men folks an' wimmens,
    'Possums ain' skace w'en dey's lots o' pu'simmons.

FROM
HOWDY, HONEY, HOWDY
1905

"Howdy, Honey, Howdy!"

Do' a-stan'in' on a jar, fiah a-shinin' thoo,
Ol' folks drowsin' 'roun' de place, wide awake is Lou,
W'en I tap, she answeh, an' I see huh 'mence to grin,
"Howdy, honey, howdy, won't you step right in?"

Den I step erpon de log layin' at de do',
Bless de Lawd, huh mammy an' huh pap's done 'menced
    to sno',
Now's de time, ef evah, ef I's gwine to try an' win,
"Howdy, honey, howdy, won't you step right in?"

No use playin' on de aidge, trimblin' on de brink,
W'en a body love a gal, tell huh whut he t'ink;
W'en huh hea't is open fu' de love you gwine to gin,
Pull yo'se'f togethah, suh, an' step right in.

Sweetes' imbitation dat a body evah hyeahed,
Sweetah den de music of a lovesick mockin'-bird,
Comin' f'om de gal you loves bettah den yo' kin,
"Howdy, honey, howdy, won't you step right in?"

At de gate o' heaven w'en de storm o' life is pas',
'Spec' I'll be a-stan'in', 'twell de Mastah say at las',
"Hyeah he stan' all weary, but he winned his fight wid sin.
Howdy, honey, howdy, won't you step right in?"

Encouragement

Who dat knockin' at de do'?
Why, Ike Johnson,—yes, fu' sho!
Come in, Ike. I's mighty glad
You come down. I t'ought you's mad

At me 'bout de othah night,
An' was stayin' 'way fu' spite.
Say, now, was you mad fu' true
W'en I kin' o' laughed at you?
    Speak up, Ike, an' 'spress yo'se'f.

'T ain't no use a-lookin' sad,
An' a-mekin' out you's mad;
Ef you's gwine to be so glum,
Wondah why you evah come.
I don't lak nobidy 'roun'
Dat jes' shet dey mouf an' frown,—
Oh, now, man, don't act a dunce!
Cain't you talk? I tol' you once,
    Speak up, Ike, an' 'spress yo'se'f.

Wha'd you come hyeah fu' to-night?
Body'd t'ink yo' haid ain't right.
I's done all dat I kin do,—
Dressed perticler, jes' fu' you;
Reckon I'd 'a' bettah wo'
My ol' ragged calico.
Aftah all the pains I's took,
Cain't you tell me how I look?
    Speak up, Ike, an' 'spress yo'se'f.

Bless my soul! I 'mos' fu'got
Tellin' you 'bout Tildy Scott.
Don't you know, come Thu'sday night,
She gwine ma'y Lucius White?
Miss Lize say I allus wuh
Heap sight laklier 'n huh;
An' she'll git me somep'n new,
Ef I wants to ma'y too.
    Speak up, Ike, an' 'spress yo'se'f.

I could ma'y in a week,
Ef de man I wants 'ud speak.
Tildy's presents'll be fine,
But dey wouldn't ekal mine.
Him whut gits me fu' a wife
'Ll be proud, you bet yo' life.
I's had offers; some ain't quit;
But I hasn't ma'ied yit!
   Speak up, Ike, an' 'spress yo'se'f.

Ike, I loves you,—yes, I does;
You's my choice, and allus was.
Laffin' at you ain't no harm.—
Go 'way, dahky, whah's yo' arm?
Hug me closer—dah, dat's right!
Wasn't you a awful sight,
Havin' me to baig you so?
Now ax whut you want to know,—
   Speak up, Ike, an' 'spress yo'se'f!

Twilight

'Twixt a smile and a tear,
   'Twixt a song and a sigh,
'Twixt the day and the dark,
   When the night draweth nigh.

Ah, sunshine may fade
   From the heavens above,
No twilight have we
   To the day of our love.

FROM *JOGGIN' ERLONG*
1906

The Capture

Duck come switchin' 'cross de lot
    Hi, oh, Miss Lady!
Hurry up an' hide de pot
    Hi, oh, Miss Lady!
Duck's a mighty 'spicious fowl,
Slick as snake an' wise as owl;
Hol' dat dog, don't let him yowl!
    Hi, oh, Miss Lady!

Th'ow dat co'n out kind o' slow
    Hi, oh, Miss Lady!
Keep yo'se'f behin' de do'
    Hi, oh, Miss Lady!
Lots o' food'll kill his feah,
Co'n is cheap but fowls is deah—
"Come, good ducky, come on heah."
    Hi, oh, Miss Lady!

Ain't he fat and ain't he fine,
    Hi, oh, Miss Lady!
Des can't wait to make him mine.
    Hi, oh, Miss Lady!
See him waddle when he walk,
'Sh! keep still and don't you talk!
Got you! Don't you daih to squawk!
    Hi, oh, Miss Lady!

UNCOLLECTED POEMS

Emancipation (1890)

Fling out your banners, your honors be bringing,
Raise to the ether your paeans of praise.
Strike every chord and let music be ringing!
Celebrate freely this day of all days.

Few are the years since that notable blessing,
Raised you from slaves to the powers of men.
Each year has seen you my brothers progressing,
Never to sink to that level again.

Perched on your shoulders sits Liberty smiling,
Perched where the eyes of the nations can see.
Keep from her pinions all contact defiling;
Show by your deeds what you're destined to be.

Press boldly forward nor waver, nor falter.
Blood has been freely poured out in your cause,
Lives sacrificed upon Liberty's altar.
Press to the front, it were craven to pause.

Look to the heights that are worth your attaining
Keep your feet firm in the path to the goal.
Toward noble deeds every effort be straining.
Worthy ambition is food for the soul!

Up! Men and brothers, be noble, be earnest!
Ripe is the time and success is assured;
Know that your fate was the hardest and sternest
When through those lash-ringing days you endured.

Never again shall the manacles gall you
Never again shall the whip stroke defame!
Nobles and Freemen, your destinies call you
Onward to honor, to glory and fame.

Welcome Address
To the Western Association of Writers

"Westward the course of empire takes its way,"—
So Berkeley said, and so to-day
The men who know the world still say.
The glowing West, with bounteous hand,
Bestows her gifts throughout the land,
And smiles to see at her command
Art, science, and the industries,—
New fruits of new Hesperides.
So, proud are you who claim the West
As home land; doubly are you blest
To live where liberty and health
Go hand in hand with brains and wealth.
So here's a welcome to you all,
Whate'er the work your hands let fall,—
To you who trace on history's page
The footprints of each passing age;
To you who tune the laureled lyre
To songs of love or deeds of fire;
To you before whose well-wrought tale
The cheek doth flush or brow grow pale;
To you who bow the ready knee
And worship cold philosophy,—
A welcome warm as Western wine,
And free as Western hearts, be thine.
Do what the greatest joy insures,—
The city has no will but yours!

Comrade

Oh, comrade, comrade, I have missed you so!
The long, drear months still lagging come and go,
And I, I strive to fill them to the brim,
But still my heart cries out, But what of him?

To-night, I sat and pored o'er pages sere,
All filled with what we did and said last year;
And all the soul within me rose and cried,
And all the woman in me sobbed and sighed.

This day we sat beside a dimpling stream,
And hours flew by like moments in a dream;
And you and I, true comrades, laughed and played,
Nor deemed it long the while we fondly stayed.

These days we stood 'neath turquoise Western sky,
And breathed new life, sipped ozone from on high;
Did mem'ry ever smile and call to thee
Those long, sweet tramps of ours, of me and thee?

Then those long dreary hours you fought with death,
And I hung near and watched your feeble breath;
And those long evening hours you clasped my hand,
And watched the twilight creeping o'er the land.

We sat upon the shore and watched the sea,
Creep higher to the rocks e'er we did flee.
And erst we angled in the dimpling bay,
And proudly counted trophies, mind'st the day?

Oh, comrade, comrade, I have missed you so!
The long drear months still lagging come and go,
And I, I strive to fill them to the brim,
But still my heart cries out, But what of him?

We've lived through sorrow and we've lived through joy,
Sweets, sweets we've tasted to our senses' cloy;
And yet we've suffered sorrow to the deep,
Full bitterness of sorrow's deadly heap.

Dost mind the books we read in other days?
Dost mind the foolish cards and little plays?
Dost mind the lilting music of our song?
Dost mind the winter eves, so sweet and long?

There is no other heart to beat with mine,
There is no other soul attuned like thine;
I miss the quick return of kindred fire,
These duller minds, oh comrade, quickly tire.

The dreary days pass on, I smile and smile,
My heart a-heavy, and soul tired the while;
The dreary nights in sleepless mis'ry creep
My soul a-cry to thine in anguish deep.

Our paths have parted, ne'er perhaps, to meet,
Your way goes west, mine east. With slow-paced feet
I take my way; yet still, again, to-night,
I pause and sob before the dreary fight.

Oh, comrade, comrade, I have missed you so!
The long drear months still lagging come and go;
And I, I strive to fill them to the brim,
But still my heart cries out, But what of him?

Love Is a Star

Love is a star that lights the night
Of life, and makes its fancies bright
As days of June with June's perfume;
A star that melts the clinging gloom
               And makes the heart's dark chambers light.

To any depth, from any height
Its light doth leap; the dusk of doom
Could not its silver trace consume
            Love is a star.

It shines undimmed, a beacon white
To Faith's unwavering, trustful sight.
'Mid warp and woof it findeth room
And weaves bright thoughts on Sorrow's loom
With lovestrung threads of pure delight.

            Love is a star.

The Making Up

Little Miss Margaret sits in a pout,
She and her Dolly have just fallen out.

Dolly is gazing with sorest stare,
Fitted dejectedly back in her chair.

Angry at Margaret, tearful and grieved,
Sore at the spanking so lately received.

Pursed are the maiden's lips close as can be,
They are not speaking, Miss Dolly and she.

Dolly unbendingly sits in her place,
Never a change coming over her face.

Up mad goes, Margaret dropping her pout,
Clasping her playmate she whispers in doubt.

Let's don't play and cry, it's too much like true,
Let's make up Dolly I ain't mad is you?

A Toast to Dayton (1917)

Love of home, sublimest passion
     That the human heart can know!
Changeless still, though fate and fashion
     Rise and fall and ebb and flow,
To the glory of our nation,
     To the welfare of our state,
Let us all with veneration
     Every effort consecrate.

And our city, shall we fail her?
     Or desert her gracious cause?
Nay—with loyalty we hail her
     And revere her righteous laws.
She shall ever claim our duty,
For she shines—the brightest gem
That has ever decked with beauty
     Dear Ohio's diadem.

Sold A C.H.S. Episode (1890)

Sing, heavenly muse, in accents tender,
This bright romance of a local fruit-vender,
How fleeting are all earthly joys!
How badly did he soak the boys!
'Tis hard to dress the thing in rhymes

And narrate how they lost their dimes;
The vender pleaded, they heard, ah, well.
The fruit, you know, was intended to sell
But only the boys (not the fruit) were sold.
They gave their money, as you've been told,
All through the day they saw at hand
Their smooth-tongued friend and his welcome stand;
All Sunday night they dreamed the same
And longed for the fruit that never came,
And Sunday eve saw that vender slick
Aboarding the train, time doubled quick,
Lament, oh muse, the wiles of men!
Farewell, ye dimes, we'll ne'er see again.

After the Struggle (1900)

Out of the blood of a conflict fraternal,
      Out of the dust and the dimness of death,
Burst into blossoms of glory eternal
Flowers that sweeten the world with their breath.
Flowers of charity, peace and devotion
      Bloom in the hearts that are empty of strife;
Love that is boundless and broad as the ocean
      Leaps into beauty and fullness of life.
So, with the singing of paeans and chorals,
      And with the flag flashing high in the sun,
Place on the graves of our heroes the laurels
      Which their unfaltering valor has won!

The Builder (1905)
To John H. Patterson, Esq.

To hue a statue from the formless stone,
To lead a regiment when death is rife,
To walk the ways of sorrow all alone
      And laugh with life,

To write a paean that a nation sings
That art must own—
     All this is life.
What is it then, to sit beside the fire,
And dream of things and idly to aspire?
To live, to struggle, nobly to desire,
     And do is life.
It is not that one needs the world's acclaim,
Brief is the sweetness of the taste of fame,
But doing, building is the nobler thing,
By which men live, and which their poets sing.
Today a builder comes, one whom we know—
A dreamer say you, of the long ago—
But, ah, the dream's fulfillment is at hand,
And all in awe of the Creator's glow,
A city's people, glad and thankful stand
To welcome one who found it good to know
And better yet to do
The things that prove man nobly great and true.

Lullaby (II)

A little brook runs where the shadows creep,
    And the whispering rushes grow,
And over the brook is the Land of Sleep,
    Where the tired children go,
And down to the water the white sheep come,
    And they nibble the tender clover,
And the children must wait in the shadows dim,
    Till all of the sheep go over.
        So it's one, two, three, and it's one, two, three,
         Counting the snow-white sheep.
       And fly away, little one, fly away, pretty one,
        Fly away to the Land of Sleep.
The little brook laughs in the moonlight fair,
    With the dancing shadows playing,
And over the bank where the daisies grow

The wayward lambs are straying.
And the children wait while the night-birds call
        From their nest in the hazel-cover,
And they count the sheep—for they must not sleep
        Till the last little lamb goes over.
The little brook hushes its rippling song
        To a tender lullaby,
And the shadows grow heavy, and deep, and long,
        And the clouds are white in the sky.
But the children have gone to the Land of Sleep,
        And sweet is the breath of the clover.
And the world lies dreaming beneath the stars,
        For the sheep have all gone over.

Index of Titles

Index of First Lines

CLICK ON A CLASSIC
www.penguinclassics.com

The world's greatest literature at your fingertips

Constantly updated information on more than a thousand titles,
from Icelandic sagas to ancient Indian epics, Russian drama to
Italian romance, American greats to African masterpieces

•

The latest news on recent additions to the list, updated
editions, and specially commissioned translations

•

Original essays by leading writers

•

A wealth of background material, including biographies
of every classic author from Aristotle to Zamyatin, plot
synopses, readers' and teachers' guides, useful web links

•

Online desk and examination copy assistance for academics

•

Trivia quizzes, competitions, giveaways, news on
forthcoming screen adaptations

James Weldon Johnson
The Autobiography of an Ex-Colored Man
Edited with an Introduction and Notes by William L. Andrews
First published in 1912, Johnson's pioneering fictional "memoir" is an unprecedented analysis of the social causes and artistic consequences of a black man's denial of his heritage.   *0-14-018402-3*

Nella Larsen
Passing
Edited with an Introduction and Notes by Thadious M. Davis
First published in 1929, this landmark novel by the Harlem Renaissance's premier woman writer candidly explores the destabilization of racial and sexual boundaries.   *0-14-243727-1*

The Portable Harlem Renaissance Reader
Edited by David Levering Lewis
This essential collection magnificently represents the greatest voices of the Harlem Renaissance with the works of Nella Larsen, Zora Neale Hurston, Langston Hughes, W. E. B. Du Bois, Richard Wright, and many more.   *0-14-017036-7*

Against Slavery: An Abolitionist Reader
Edited and with an Introduction by Mason Lowance
An original anthology of primary documents from the eighteenth- and nineteenth-century antislavery and abolitionist movements, including speeches, lectures, and essays by Garrison, Douglass, Emerson, and Lydia Maria Child.   *0-14-043758-4*

Sojourner Truth
Narrative of Sojourner Truth
Edited with an Introduction and Notes by Nell Irvin Painter
Sojourner Truth's landmark narrative, dictated to a neighbor, chronicles her experiences as a slave in upstate New York and her transformation into a well-known abolitionist, feminist, orator, and preacher. This unique volume is based on the most complete text, the 1884 edition of the *Narrative*.   *0-14-043678-2*

Booker T. Washington
Up from Slavery
Introduction by Louis R. Harlan
Washington's autobiography reveals the conviction he held that the black man's salvation lay in education, industriousness, and self-reliance. 0-14-039051-0

Phillis Wheatley
Complete Writings
Edited and with an Introduction and Notes by Vincent Carretta
This volume collects the astonishing writings of the eighteenth-century American slave who published her first poem at the age of fourteen. It includes her letters, poetry, hymns, elegies, translations, tales, and epyllions. 0-14-042430-X

William Wells Brown
Clotel: Or, The President's Daughter
Edited with an Introduction and Notes by M. Giulia Fabi
First published in 1853, Clotel was written amid then unconfirmed rumors that Thomas Jefferson had fathered children with one of his slaves. A fast-paced and harrowing tale, *Clotel* is a founding text of the African American novelist tradition, a brilliantly composed and richly detailed exploration of human relations in a new world in which race is a cultural construct. 0-14-243772-7

Charles W. Chesnutt
Conjure Tales and Stories of the Color Line
Edited with an Introduction by William L. Andrews
Chesnutt probed psychological depths in black people previously unheard of in Southern regional writing. This important collection brings together all the stories in his two published volumes, *The Conjure Woman* and *The Wife of His Youth*, along with two uncollected works: "Dave's Neckliss" and "Baxter's Procustes." 0-14-118502-3

Frederick Douglass
Narrative of the Life of Frederick Douglass, an American Slave
Edited with an Introduction by Houston A. Baker, Jr.
The preeminent example of the American slave narrative, Douglass's personal account of life in the pre–Civil War American South is a telling indictment of the institution of slavery and of the people and the country that allowed it to flourish.   *0-14-039012-X*

W. E. B. Du Bois
The Souls of Black Folk
Introduction by Donald B. Gibson and Notes by Monica M. Elbert
Social reformer and activist W. E. B. Du Bois expresses his passionate concern for the future of his race in this 1903 collection of essays depicting the psychological effects of segregation on American society. This classic exploration of the moral and intellectual issues surrounding the perception of blacks within American society remains an important document of our social and political history.
1-14-018998-X

Olaudah Equiano
The Interesting Narrative and Other Writings
Edited with an Introduction and Notes by Vincent Carretta
An account of the slave trade by a former slave and loyal British subject, *The Interesting Narrative* is both an exciting, often terrifying, adventure story and an important precursor to such famous nineteenth-century slave narratives as Frederick Douglass's autobiography. This revised and expanded edition includes twice the number of previously known published and unpublished works by Equiano.   *0-14-243716-6*

Harriet Jacobs
Incidents in the Life of a Slave Girl: Written by Herself
Edited with an Introduction and Notes by Nell Irvin Painter
Jacobs's haunting, evocative memoir of her life as a slave in North Carolina and her final escape and emancipation is one of the most important books ever written documenting the traumas and horrors of slavery—and the particular experiences of female slaves—in the antebellum South. This edition also includes "A True Tale of Slavery," written by Jacobs's brother, John, for a London periodical.
0-14-043795-9

FOR THE BEST IN PAPERBACKS, LOOK FOR THE

In every corner of the world, on every subject under the sun, Penguin represents quality and variety—the very best in publishing today.

For complete information about books available from Penguin—including Penguin Classics, Penguin Compass, and Puffins—and how to order them, write to us at the appropriate address below. Please note that for copyright reasons the selection of books varies from country to country.

In the United States: Please write to *Penguin Putnam Inc., P.O. Box 12289 Dept. B, Newark, New Jersey 07101-5289* or call 1-800-788-6262.

In the United Kingdom: Please write to *Dept. EP, Penguin Books Ltd, Bath Road, Harmondsworth, West Drayton, Middlesex UB7 0DA.*

In Canada: Please write to *Penguin Books Canada Ltd, 10 Alcorn Avenue, Suite 300, Toronto, Ontario M4V 3B2.*

In Australia: Please write to *Penguin Books Australia Ltd, P.O. Box 257, Ringwood, Victoria 3134.*

In New Zealand: Please write to *Penguin Books (NZ) Ltd, Private Bag 102902, North Shore Mail Centre, Auckland 10.*

In India: Please write to *Penguin Books India Pvt Ltd, 11 Panchsheel Shopping Centre, Panchsheel Park, New Delhi 110 017.*

In the Netherlands: Please write to *Penguin Books Netherlands bv, Postbus 3507, NL-1001 AH Amsterdam.*

In Germany: Please write to *Penguin Books Deutschland GmbH, Metzlerstrasse 26, 60594 Frankfurt am Main.*

In Spain: Please write to *Penguin Books S. A., Bravo Murillo 19, 1° B, 28015 Madrid.*

In Italy: Please write to *Penguin Italia s.r.l., Via Benedetto Croce 2, 20094 Corsico, Milano.*

In France: Please write to *Penguin France, Le Carré Wilson, 62 rue Benjamin Baillaud, 31500 Toulouse.*

In Japan: Please write to *Penguin Books Japan Ltd, Kaneko Building, 2-3-25 Koraku, Bunkyo-Ku, Tokyo 112.*

In South Africa: Please write to *Penguin Books South Africa (Pty) Ltd, Private Bag X14, Parkview, 2122 Johannesburg.*